JAMES' JOURNEY

JIM & SHERRY HOWELL, EDITED BY BARBARA HOWELL

PUBLISHED BY FASTPENCIL, INC.

Published by FastPencil, Inc.
3131 Bascom Ave.
Suite 150
Campbell CA 95008 USA
(408) 540-7571
(408) 540-7572 (Fax)
info@fastpencil.com
http://www.fastpencil.com

Throughout this manuscript only first names of many friends are used; this is done for their privacy. However, credit certainly goes to Dr. Reddy, Dr. Shavati, and Dr. Jharus.

First Edition

This manuscript is dedicated to James Howell, a wonderful little boy who has shown, and continues to show, courage in fighting the dreaded disease, cancer. Also, to the many boys and girls that are in this same struggle. May God bless and be with each and every one.

Acknowledgements

This manuscript could not have been created without the parents, Jim and Sherry, willing to share their experiences when faced with their 4 1/2 year old son's dreaded diagnosis of cancer. Their dedication in documenting their daily experiences with James is what created this manuscript. Also, the precious love of Allison, the best big sister a boy could have. Thanks to the many relatives and friends that have been, and still are, right there when needed. Thank you to the wonderful doctors, nurses and medical personnel at Children's Hospital in Birmingham, Alabama, especially Clinic 8 and 4 Tower, and The University of Alabama at Birmingham, who give tirelessly of their talents for so many.

Also, many thanks to Michael Ashley at FastPencil for his help and confidence as I tried my hand at publishing.

CONTENTS

1

INTRODUCTION

This manuscript, "James' Journey" is a grandmother's attempt at sharing, not only his story of courage, but his family and friends story of love shared, inspiration, companionship, and cultivation of new friends that were born and grew through this little boy's battle with cancer.

The story is told from the many entries over a 4 year period* that his father and mother shared through a website, CaringBridge. CaringBridge is a "free, personalized website that connects loved ones during critical illness, treatment and recovery." It is being offered in the hope that it will help others that may be facing the challenge of that dreaded diagnosis, cancer. May it help others as they read of James' treatment, his daily experiences, both good and bad, as well as that of his family and friends.

Our hope is that his story may reach someone that needs to have their faith renewed by "walking" with this family through their journey.....which still continues today.

Credits: Throughout this manuscript only first names of many friends are used; this is done for their privacy. However, credit certainly goes to Dr. Reddy, Dr. Satchivi, Dr. Jharus, Dr. Brown and Dr. Hamm.

*This manuscript begins October 2005 through August 2006. James' journey will continue in an additional manuscript.

2

James' Journey

October is really a beautiful month in Birmingham, Alabama.

The mountain sides are glorious with the leaves turning red, gold and orange. But, on this Friday in mid-October morning my thoughts were not with the surroundings around me. Even though it was a beautiful drive downtown, on this particular morning this grandmother was on her way to meet Sherry (daughter-in-law) and James (4 ½ year old grandson) at Children's Hospital for an MRI that had been scheduled by a doctor at UAB. This MRI was just to confirm that the recent diagnosis of "lazy eye" was just that and that nothing else was wrong. James' mother had noticed that his eye had begun to turn in slightly and that he sometimes said he could see "two of her." Very wisely, the parents, after consultation from Dr. Charles Brown, followed up on this and a very conscious doctor at

UAB wanted an MRI before scheduling the surgery necessary to repair the "lazy eye."

Since this was just supposed to be a routine test, again just doing a check by the eye doctor at UAB since the eye surgery was to be scheduled the following week, only James' mother (Sherry) was with him. His sister (Allison) was at school, father (Jim) at work and this was going to be a quick procedure.

I met Sherry in the MRI waiting room and she said James was a trooper, took the needle in the vein fairly well and was sound asleep awaiting the procedure. We were all optimistic about the test; after all James was a little boy that appeared healthy, very handsome, bright and full of life. However, when the radiologist walked into that small waiting room Sherry and I both knew by the look in his eyes that we needed to brace ourselves for some bad news. With a very kind voice, filled with some emotion, he told us that our little boy had a brain tumor and it was most likely malignant. At that moment our entire lives changed. Somehow we managed to telephone for his Dad and Grandfather (called DJ for DaddyJack) to come to the hospital. The doctor that delivered the news said a team of doctors would want to meet with us as soon as possible.

The first meeting with Dr. Satchivi and his team of 2 other professionals was traumatic. I do remember their kindness and concern and when James' father looked into Dr. Satchivi's eyes and asked him if he had children and if he was a Christian. His answer was "I'm expecting my first in a few months and yes I am a Christian." He and his team explained that the surgery was needed as soon as possible and it was scheduled for the following Monday.

This is the beginning of James' journey, and that of his family. I cannot give his story the credit it deserves, but through his parents', family members, friends and strangers that later become some of the most endeared friends, there is a journal that Jim and Sherry created, not only to tell his story, but God working through them, has given them the strength and courage to walk the miles with the dreaded disease called cancer, and also has been an inspiration for many people meeting the challenges of sickness. It is because of the many people that have been touched, inspired, and some have said it has changed their lives, that I give you James' story, which is written from the hearts of his parents. Claiming no literary experience, it is truly from the heart.

Their journal is a beautiful story of courage, hardships endured, lessons learned, and most of all that by the grace of God, all things are possible.

3

The Journal and Journey Begins

October, 2005

Jesus said, "With men this is impossible, but with God, all things are possible." Matthew 19:26

James is our 4 ½ -year old son. He was diagnosed with medulloblastoma 10/21/05 and our entire world changed. He had brain surgery 10/24 to remove the tumor that was causing pressure on his 5th & 6th optic nerves. We spend the week at Children's Hospital in Birmingham, AL and were released 10/28. When we arrived home, I opened the car door and he said, "Dad, I sure am glad to be home."

We go back to Children's 11/8 for another MRI on his spine. The doctors say this cancer tends to "drip" and they want to check him out. November 9 has James getting a spinal tap and port. Radiation and chemo aren't options, they're necessities. We are in for a marathon, not a sprint and while we know a lot, we still don't know anything.

We have trusted in Christ and have turned this over to him. We still have our moments, but we know, only through the eyes of Jesus, James will be cured.

Family and friends have come together for us and we are truly blessed. We can't thank them enough for the support. Everyone asks, "What can we do?" and our answer is simple. Please pray. Prayer is his hope and salvation, as well as ours. Sherry, Allison (James' 9 year old sister) and I remember this and find the burden less when we talk with Jesus. Please continue the prayer lists. If he isn't on one, please place him. Prayers are mighty powerful and we have seen them answered. I told my wife that James is in a win/win situation. He either comes home with us, or he goes home with Jesus. We have been blessed to have him for 4 ½ years and we look forward to him growing up. Through the eyes of God our son will be cured. Please continue to pray and may God bless my son, my family and friends, and you.

In Christ,

Jim

Monday, November 7, 2005 – 10:12 p.m.

Hello everyone—

Tomorrow is a big day for us – pray for no cancer on the spine!! When we get the results tomorrow we will post those on the internet, but I bet it will be late, 8:00 or 9:00 p.m. I can hardly breathe much less go to sleep but I know I need to have rest and have a clear mind to listen to what the doctors are about to tell us.

James is sleeping peacefully in my bed and has had a great day! He knows he has to go back to the hospital tomorrow for a picture of his spine and is okay with that, but he said, "NO shots Mommy." This broke my heart but it is only the beginning….Please keep James in your prayers and on as many prayer lists as possible. Thanks for all your love and support.

Keep praying for my "Little Man,"
Sherry

TUESDAY, NOVEMBER 8, 2005 – 9:25 P.M.

Praise Jesus! Prayers are working, so please keep them up! Just got the news – NOTHING on the spine!!! Dr. Reddy said everything looked great and she was very happy with his progress. Dr. Satchivi (surgeon) sat in and said he couldn't be more pleased with James. He said his scar was better than he had hoped. Dr. Reddy told James to run down the hall and before she could say go, he bee-lined to me. James wasn't happy with getting stuck with the needle, but he is tough. It took the max dosage of medicine to knock him out for the MRI. The nurse had to call the doctor to up the amount.

We have crossed a major hurdle, and we are blessed. We go back at 9:30 a.m. for the tap and port. Please keep the prayers coming for more good news. The news we get tomorrow determines Dr. Reddy's course of action, but we are just thankful for the news tonight.

We are staying strong with our faith in Jesus and we will keep fighting. James is my hero and pal and he's much tougher than any of us. Thank you all for the thoughts and prayers, please don't stop. Special thanks to Angela (Child Life Specialist) and "Clay" for the much needed help. (Clay is a special little doll with his special ventriloquist Angela). There are ANGELS all around us. For now, we are going to bed; we are in for a long day tomorrow.

In Christ,

Jim

WEDNESDAY, NOVEMBER 9, 2005 – 9:45 P.M.

The good Lord gave us another day, for that we are thankful. James came through the port and spinal tap great. (Note: Magic milk is term used for anesthesia administered via the noodle and port. The noodle is a tube-like vial that is connected to the port. The port is a device which is used to deliver medications into the bloodstream. The port is completely implanted beneath the skin and is visible merely as a small raised area beneath the skin. The small raised area is where a needle is inserted for delivery of the medication. James' port is in his upper chest) we won't know 100% results from the tap until tomorrow, but the doctor was encouraged by the fluid. She said it was clear and had no blood. Sounded great, but we will have to wait. Once again, prayers are being answered. It was a long day, but we made it. We got to the hospital at 9:30 a.m., didn't go to surgery until 1:20 p.m. but he never complained; he was hungry and thirsty, but never a word. He is tough. We made it home around 6:15 p.m.; we did get some instructions on the port but have nothing definitive until the results are 100% on the tap. We go back Monday for more, but we are going to enjoy the weekend. Thanks again to family, friends and especially the doctors and nurses for their love and caring ways. A special thanks to Angela and "Clay." You made a very tough and long day much easier on the 1 and 2 most special people in our lives. Bless you.

Until we have more news…please keep praying.

Jim

THURSDAY, NOVEMBER 10, 2005 – 6:45 P.M.

Jesus said, "With men this is impossible, but with God, all things are possible." Matthew 19:26

We just got another miracle…no cancer in the spinal fluid. Praise the Lord! We have been blessed with Thursday; we had to wait until 4:00 p.m., but the news came and we are thankful. I never thought I would be thankful for radiation and chemo, but maybe now the dosage will be smaller. It is indeed great news and we will go Monday to begin the "fight for my pal." James met me at the door this afternoon and said, "Dad, my cancer isn't there." Words we have been praying for. From the initial report on James to now, miracles have happened. Sherry called Allison at dance practice and told her the news. I have a feeling there was an extra bounce in her step.

Once again the fight has just started and Dr. Reddy can now set us a course. We should find out our plan for a cure on Monday. Until then, we will enjoy every day the Lord will grant us.

Please hug your kids extra tonight or tell that someone you love them. We all are on loan from Jesus. We just want to keep our "lease" on James for a long time. Please keep praying. He needs them, we need them. We will continue ours. Thanks to all of you who have taken the time to visit this site, CaringBridge. The messages are appreciated and we can feel His power through all of you. There are no strangers. Thank you doesn't seem enough, but for now, it's what we have. Please keep His power coming.

In Christ,

Jim

MONDAY, NOVEMBER 14, 2005 – 9:15 P.M.

Hello everyone – we made it through another hurdle, getting our port accessed (needle inserted into the port) today!!! We met with the group of radiologists today and then a hearing test (we passed). We then made our way to Children's (Hospital) to get our port accessed. James was such a trooper and only cried for 2 minutes. Clay and Angela (Child Life Specialist) always find us and show up at the right time. Thanks go out to Anne and Andrew who shared their wonderful secret with us about the no stick tape—it was so wonderful and truly helped the situation of getting stuck! We love you guys so much already. Tomorrow we go to the tumor center and get molds of our head and body made, and a cat scan. James will be sedated and the procedure will take 2 to 3 hours. Pray for another good day and that James keeps up his sweet spirit. Keep praying for my "little man,"

Sherry

TUESDAY, NOVEMBER 15, 2005 – 8:41 P.M.

No one said it would be easy and today was one of those days. We went to the tumor center and James was terrified of being put to sleep. We had "magic milk" for the first time and boy does it work fast! He had all his molds made and the CAT scan, and while he was asleep they flushed his port and took off all the syringes. When we got home an hour later we got a phone call that the scan didn't look clear enough and we needed to do it all over again in the morning at 7:00. This will mean going to Children's in the morning and getting stuck again in our port and then back to the tumor center. I know this seems very minor but James is still so scared of all the needles and it is very hard to watch your child be that scared. Please continue to pray that with every visit it gets easier for my precious "little man." I'm told that within weeks sometimes months he won't even cry when he gets stuck. Can't wait for those days. Thanks for all the love and support we continue to receive daily.

Sherry

SUNDAY, NOVEMBER 20, 2005 – 8:06 P.M.

Tomorrow is another big day. We start at 6:30 a.m. and access his port. We have our first radiation treatment at 7:30 a.m. We aren't sure how long it will take. He's doing great. If you saw him you would never know anything was going on. James isn't looking forward to tomorrow, but the folks at Hand-in-Paw will be there to help out. (Hand-in-Paw is a non-profit organization of trained teams of handlers and their animals that help people heal both physically and emotionally). We do radiation Tuesday and chemo thrown in as well. We will have Thanksgiving off, but go back Friday for a treatment. This is one Thanksgiving that we will cherish. We are blessed to have him and will take it one day at a time.

Please keep James in your prayers. We need every one of them. It's funny; we thought the brain surgery was tough. It seems like a walk in the park compared to tomorrow. We are looking at it like this; it's one day closer for the radiation and chemo to be over. People have asked about Angela and "Clay." She is a Child Life Specialist and has been blessed as a ventriloquist. "Clay" is her special friend and gets James to understand all that is happening. She has been a blessing. We can't thank her or our family and friends enough for their support.

That's all we have for now. Please pray for a great outcome. We are

In Christ,

Jim

Tuesday, November 22, 2005 – 9:27 p.m.

"Do you believe that I am able to do this?" Matthew 9:28

"Is anything too hard for me?" Jer. 32:27

This is what we believe with every fiber of our bodies. James is the bravest and toughest person I know. He hasn't complained, he has fussed when he gets uncomfortable, but he takes what they give him. We started a chemo round in with the radiation. James showed some after effects from the chemo. His jaw and some of his joints are hurting, but he is tough.

We are looking forward to Thanksgiving. We have much to be thankful for, great and loving family and friends. James will have his five cousins from Chicago and one from Louisville in this weekend. I hope he is up for it. We know tomorrow will be tougher because of the chemo, but this is our path. We hope everyone has a safe and peaceful holiday. Please be careful.

Go with this: Nothing is too hard for Jesus. No man can work like him. Thank you Mrs. Dunn for the book. You were right, it helps. We know the prayers are working. Thanks to all who are praying and please keep them up.

In Christ,

Jim

FRIDAY, NOVEMBER 25, 2005 – 9:34 A.M.

"Be still, and know that I am God" (Psalm 45:10)

This verse works so well for James when he has radiation. Seeing his little body lying on the table after his "magic milk" is hard, but the Lord is caring for our son. Our hearts are heavy, but you can feel the peace of God working through the doctors and tech folks. They are all so caring and their skill is evident. They make James feel at ease, and we notice this. We've finished our first week and James is happy to have his "noodle" removed. We will enjoy the weekend.

Thanksgiving was great. Having family around is the best medicine for James. You can see it in his eyes, and he forgets all that is going on with the treatments. We are blessed to have such a strong family. Combine that with friends and prayers, we are blessed. Continued thanks for all of the support. We rely on the prayers, they get us through each day. Please keep James close to your heart. He and his sister are rays of sunshine for us.

In Christ,

Jim

MONDAY, NOVEMBER 28, 2008 – 8:05 P.M.

"I am with you all the day, Rejoice"

Another early day for James, he is such a trooper. At the hospital Sherry commented on how lucky we were. There are so many sick children. At least we get to sleep in our bed at night. Accessing the port was a little better today. He still doesn't like it, but it was tolerated. He took a step closer to not having the "magic milk" for radiation. It will come. He is getting a little more familiar with everything. James made it to school for an hour today. Slowly, we are trying to get back to normal.

Thanksgiving spent with family was the best medicine for James and Allison. They love being with the Chicago clan. I think it helped them as well. We are looking forward to the "Season of Miracles." We are keeping our faith strong, and we know James will be cured. "Nothing is impossible with God."(Luke 1:37).

Thanks to everyone for the wonderful support. Give your kids an extra hug and please don't forget to say, "I love you."

In Christ,

Jim

FRIDAY, DECEMBER 2, 2005 – 1:27 P.M.

Say to the faint hearted: "Be strong; do not fear" (Isaiah 35:4)

This is James. He to me as we left this morning, "Dad, I'm going to do what they (Children's Hospital nurses) ask so we can come home."

We wrapped up another week (thank you Lord). James is upbeat and continues to amaze us. He was hurting behind his ear and head before. Let's pray this continues – 22 more radiation treatments left!

We have a big weekend coming up. James is riding the fire truck in the Christmas parade along with other kids. I hope he feels strong enough. 36-48 hours after chemo are "iffy".

Thanks for the prayers and support. We need all we can get. Remember, love on your kids. They are on loan to us.

In Christ,

Jim

TUESDAY, DECEMBER 6, 2005 – 9:14 P.M.

"Sing…to the Lord, always giving thanks to God the Father for everything." (Ephesians 5:19-20)

We have seen the source of evil confronting us, but we know God is surrounding and protecting James. He is going on his 3rd great week. We are blessed that the treatments are "routine." James wakes up with a smile and is ready for a new day. The challenges are many, but he will prevail. James is not alone. You can feel the power of Jesus and the prayers that are flowing for James.

James went to the Christmas parade and rode the fire truck Saturday morning. The firemen were great. He had a great time on the truck and being at the station. He was tired later in the day, but he played with his buddies at a birthday party. It was wonderful to see him running around.

We have 20 more radiations and another chemo tomorrow. They keep throwing things at him and he keeps hitting them out of the park. His toughness is amazing. Saturday morning Sherry said, "I don't want to jinx this, but he is doing great." I told her, jinx had nothing to do with it; it is the power of prayer lifting him up. His hair is beginning to fall out, but he is ready. We have talked about it, and it is gong to bother mom and dad more than him. He really is my pal and my hero.

People ask if we are ok. It is not easy, and I will not lie, but we are at peace. When you turn it over to Jesus, He takes over. I know He can take care of James better than me, and that is how I face the day. We will take what the Lord gives us tomorrow and be thankful.

Keep your kids close to your heart. They are a blessing. The Season of Miracles is upon us. Please continue the love and prayers, they are working. We rely on the strength of all of you to face the day and we give our thanks to the Lord for everything.

In Christ,
Jim

SATURDAY, DECEMBER 10, 2005 – 12:06 P.M.

"Our light and momentary troubles are achieving to us an eternal glory that far outweighs them all." (2 Corinthians 4:17)

I understand there will be sorrow in our lives, but the sadness itself produces the reward. It teaches us how precious life is.

James is through another week. He's at the plate and he isn't taking any pitches. He's swinging away. He is a remarkable little boy. The treatments are a part of him, and he understands the process. The radiation folks have fallen in love with him, and what is not to love? We finished the overall brain and spine treatments. Starting Monday they concentrate on the tumor bed with radiation. He will get a more powerful dose, so we will take it as it comes. The "Hand-in-Paw" folks make it better and he looks forward to their visits. Please keep James in your prayers as the new treatments start. 17 more to go!

I said earlier that life is precious, and what is the reward? It was this morning as I got up early to do errands. James woke up and wanted to go with me. I was so thankful to have my "pal" with me. The little things that Jesus gives us grow big. You just have to look and he is getting me to do that. James' hair is about gone now so the hats and bandanas are on! It does get cold in Alabama when you have no hair! I never realized, until now. (Jim has shaved his head and will continue to do so as long as James has no hair)

Thank you for all the support and prayers. We are blessed to have such wonderful family and friends to call upon. We get meals from people we don't know, but the love and prayers of strangers are strong. Sherry and I didn't know how wonderful the meals would be, but they give us more time to spend with James and Allison. A huge "thank you" to all the cooks and the people that organize. Thanks to the Sims family. Dan, you make this situation go better with your foundation for Janie. Thanks for letting us lean on you. (Dan is the founder of the Janie Sims Foundation. His young daughter lost her battle with cancer.)

This season is magical. You can feel the warmth of Christ as this day grows closer. Give your family extra love tonight.

In Christ,

Jim

TUESDAY, DECEMBER 13, 2005 – 11:43 A.M.

"Commit your way to the Lord; trust in Him and He will do this." (Psalm 37.5)

Another treatment is done – 15 more. We are on the down slope now and James continues his journey. I don't know how people get through rough times without Christ. If we had not turned this over to Him on day one, we would be exhausted. We "roll" our burdens to Him and while our faith is tested, He works and His word is true.

James lost a pound last week. We have to get him eating some high calories, or he may have to start a steroid. The doctors aren't concerned yet, but James has to do something. His attitude is great and everything seems to be on track. His radiation is more concentrated and he looses steam pretty fast. He is excited about the season and loves to "shop" with Granma and DJ. We can't do this without family and friends. The guestbook (Caringbridge) helps us a lot. I'm very happy that it may be helping you and your family. This is a very special time, please enjoy those moments and cherish them. Please keep the prayers coming, we need every one.

In Christ,

Jim

Friday, December 16, 2005 – 8:54 p.m.

"Everyone who calls on the name of the Lord will be saved." (Joel 2:23)

Trust, is what we must do. This has been a tougher week. 12 more radiations to go and James is getting a little tired of the process. After the treatment he is ready to go home. He doesn't want to be messed with and I don't blame him. The radiation is concentrating on the tumor bed and is a more intense does. He still isn't eating with consistency. However, this morning he had tater tots, ice cream and sprite. We don't care what it is as long as it's high in calories and fat. It seems his tastes change hourly. That is tough. I wish I could take this cancer from him, and one day I will understand. Coach Evans (high school coach and friend) said one day that James and I will call on this for strength, and we would understand. He's right, but it's still tough.

James watched his sister in her school Christmas play. He then played with his friend, Evan, in the gym. It was wonderful to see them running around. I'll keep saying, love your kids, they are on loan. James is getting excited about Christmas and the one thing that is helping is Angel. She is the family dog of his Chicago cousins; they left her with us on their Thanksgiving visit. James says, "Dad, Angel helps with my cancer." It's obvious. Anything that helps is ok with me.

I pray for my son and I thank all of you for yours. Please continue and let the strength of Christ bless all of us this season.

In Christ,

Jim

WEDNESDAY, DECEMBER 21, 2005 – 3:37 P.M.

"I am not alone, for my Father is with me." (John 16:32)

We are now in the single digits for radiation – 9 left. The doctors are very pleased with James' progress. The radiologist says James is the model for what they are going for with treatment. Wonderful words to hear and Christ gets all of the credit. Through Him, His love and caring shows through the doctors. Next Wednesday is the last chemo until February. We will end the radiation January 4 or 5. We look forward to the time off. Dr. Reddy is extremely pleased with his progress. She is wonderful, as well as everyone on her team and the radiology team. We are blessed to have these folks on our side.

We are looking forward to Christmas. Obviously, this year will be looked upon in a different way. Please don't take you family or friends for granted. You may not talk with everyone on a daily basis, but keep them in your heart. Make everyday you are given the best. That is what we are trying to do. Through our Lord we draw strength. Merry Christmas to everyone and thank you all for the prayers. We are a very lucky family to have all of this wonderful support…

In Christ,

Jim

SATURDAY, DECEMBER 24, 2005 - 10:31 A.M.

"And the angel said unto them. Fear not: for, behold I bring you good tidings of great joy, which shall be to all people. For unto you is born this day in the city of David a Saviour, which is Christ the Lord." (Luke 2:10-11)

For this, my family is blessed. This is the best Christmas we've ever had. My family is together and we are closer than ever, and I am thankful. We've told some of this story, but here it is. …..When we got home from the hospital the Friday after surgery, James told Sherry about a dream he had in the hospital. A little history first. My great-uncle, Henry, was 96 years old when he passed a few months ago. He lived in Jackson, AL down the road from my grandmother's home. We would visit and James and Allison loved seeing him. Tiffany was our dog for 14 years. She died before James was born. He also never knew Sherry's Mom, Grandma B, she died at age 52 before James was born.

That night James was holding Sherry's face in his hands and said, "Mom, you've got pretty eyes." She said, "Thank you, I've got eyes like you." He said, "I know where they came from, Jesus gave them to me. He's in my heart Mom. He made me, you, sissy and daddy." Sherry said, "You're right, how did you get to be so smart?" He said, "Jesus told me. He was in the hospital and He took me to heaven. He was holding my hand and He was walking. We saw Uncle Henry and he was sitting in his chair. He wasn't saying anything; he was just smiling at me. And, Tiffany was running around like a crazy dog. I didn't see Grandma B but Jesus said she was there. Mom, it was pretty there, there were lots of toys and playgrounds and it was nice. I asked Him if I could go home and He said, "Okay." Mom, Jesus is in my heart." Sherry and I cried. Our son walked with Him. It's a wonderful feeling to know Christ is taking care of James. We know He can do it better than us and we know the prayers are working. I've said before, this is the Season of Miracles, and we get them everyday.

James has 7 radiations left. We have a chemo next Wednesday and Dr. Reddy said we have no more until February. The countdown is on! It will be a welcomed break. James needs it. He is looking forward to Santa and he will have a big surprise tomorrow, as well as Allison. We want to thank our family, friends and those we don't know. Please continue to lift up in your prayers. We need every one of them.

May God's blessings shine down upon all of you. Sherry and I tell each other how lucky we are to have such a wonderful support group. We are the lucky ones and we can feel the prayers and love everyday. From my family to yours, let Jesus into your heart every second and have a Merry Christmas. I know this family will.

In Christ,

Jim

WEDNESDAY, DECEMBER 28, 2005 – 7:47 P.M.

"The Lord will fulfill his purpose for me."(Psalm 138:8)

We have total faith that James will be healed. Jesus is in control; you can feel His power.

James is down to 5 radiations. We will be finished with them January 4, 2006. We took the last chemo today until February 1st. Dr. Reddy said he looked great. His coordination was wonderful. She said she didn't need to see him until the 1st. James will have an MRI, a new round of chemo and other tests. We will spend the night and see where we go next on this journey.

Christmas was the best ever. We have to thank the Chicago family for a special gift. When they came to visit Thanksgiving they were to come back Christmas, so they left their dog, Angel with us; she was so good for James. On Christmas day they phoned; they were unable to come back as previously planned due to a stomach bug and they knew they could not be around James, so their phone message was that Angel was ours to keep. Angel is a Bichon, and as I write this, she is curled up by James in the bed.

James and Allison were so excited. Angel is so sweet and James said, "Dad, she makes me feel good, she helps me with my cancer." She knows something is going on with James and anything that will comfort him, I'm for. It was a great surprise and a great Christmas gift. Santa was great to James; he brought him a bike. We have been loving the warm weather. Getting James outside now is wonderful.

We continue to ask for your thoughts and prayers. We can't do this alone. Prayers are helping and we need to start them now for great news from the February MRI. James has tolerated the chemo and radiation well. He actually gained a ½ lb after losing weight for 2 weeks. His tastes continue to change, but we'll find something he will eat. One day at a time.

God's blessings on everyone for the New Year.

In Christ,

Jim

MONDAY, JANUARY 2, 2006 – 2:24 P.M.

"Surely I am with you always." (Matthew 28:20)

Happy New Year to all. This year will be different, that is for sure. We know we don't have to worry about tomorrow, because the Lord watched us today. We know He won't forget about us.

We have 3 more radiations which we will start Tuesday. The doctors said that missing 3 days will not hurt. Dr. Jharus said as long as James wasn't sick, we were ok. We will take January off. We then go on 9 chemo cycles every 6 weeks. February 1 starts us on another journey. We keep reminding ourselves of what Dr. Shatavi said; we are in for a marathon, not a sprint. As long as James handles the chemo, we will take them in stride. Our concern in his weight. His tastes have changed so much. It's tough to watch. He spent New Years night at Granma's and DJ's. He would not eat well there and I think that is a first at her house for anyone! He did put on the rally cap once he came home.

Thank you so much for the prayers and thoughts on this site (Caringbridge). We love to read the guest book. It keeps your heart warm knowing the love is flowing. God has a special plan for our "littleman." We don't know the long term, but he (James) has touched many in the short term. We've known how special James is, and now we get to share. Thank you all for the love. Please continue to keep James in your hearts. He has Jesus in his.

In Christ,

Jim

THURSDAY, JANUARY 5, 2005 – 9:36 P.M.

Jesus replied, "You may go. Your son will live" The man took Jesus at his word and departed (John 4:50)

Wow, does this cover us or what? It is what we believe. Radiation OVER! Needless to say, we are happy. James was counting down the days. Today, Brooke, the technician that gives him "magic milk" asked, "James, how many more?" He didn't hold any fingers up, just his fist. Everyone at radiation is wonderful. They have made a very difficult situation bearable. I can't tell you how helpless you are when your child is put to sleep. I thought it would get easier, but I always walked out of the room with a tear in my eye. James got used to it. He would go in the room and turn the light off (for the technician). He would then hold up his "noodle" for the medicine. He is so brave. We can't thank the radiation folks enough. The love and care shown to our son was felt. We knew he was in good hands. The Lord has truly blessed these folks. They are special.

We are going to rest for a while. James did say he wanted to go to school to see his buddies. We did celebrate tonight; Lindsey (age 5) and James went to a movie and dinner together. It was their first date. He brought flowers; always works. They are very cute together. Maybe now we can get him around some folks his age.

We still have to watch his resistance. It's low and his weight is still an issue. Dr.Jharus said he should feel much better in a week or so and his appetite should return. We will enjoy the time off and get him stronger for the next round.

We have the James' bracelets in. Let us know if you would like one. The money will go to the foundation. They are green, his favorite color and have his name on them, as well as Matthew 19:26.

Thank you everyone for getting him through this first part. The prayers are sill needed and appreciated. We are trusting in our Lord and staying strong.

"Whatever you ask for in prayer, believe." (Mark 11:24)

In Christ,

Jim

THURSDAY, JANUARY 12, 2006 – 8:11 P.M.

"Trust in the Lord with all you heart and lean not on your own understanding." (Proverbs 3:5)

It's been a week since James' last radiation and sleep has been the order of the day. He is catching up; his appetite is improving, just not fast enough for us. As parents we are impatient, but we have to "trust." James made it to school for a little while this week, he just doesn't have much stamina. We are confident it will come. He is a strong little boy and has taught me much since this started. He has a great attitude. He told me the other day, "Dad, I miss the "magic milk" people, but I don't miss the "noodle" ones." He is great.

Thanks to all who sign the guest book (at Caring-Bridge). We tell James everyday that many people are praying and thinking of him and we read him the entries. Please continue the prayers, we need them all. Pray for him to gain weight; he's going to need the extra pounds for the next treatment round. Thanks to all and please continue to "trust in Him."

Praying for James,

Jim

WEDNESDAY, JANUARY 18, 2006 – 6:35 P.M.

"Ask and it will be given to you; seek and you will find; knock and the door will be opened to you. For everyone who asks receives; he who seeks finds; and to him who knocks, the door will be opened." (Matthew 7:7-8)

James had a checkup yesterday with Dr. Jharus. They thought he looked great. We think he's losing weight.

They said that food may be an issue for him, meaning, with all that has happened to him in the past few months, eating the one thing he can control. The doctors give him a mild (and nasty tasting) steroid for 5 days, so we will see. They commented on how active he was and how he did not look lethargic. I guess we see our little boy in a different light and they see so many kids who are much worse than us. Once again, we are blessed. It's all per-spective. We are loving the time off and James gets a little stronger each day. He has the desire to get outside and to play indoors, but his stamina isn't there yet. He asked the other day if he could play baseball this year, and as long as the doctors say yes, we will give it a shot.

Thanks to all for the support on the bracelets for James. For those asking for them, they are coming to you. If anyone would like one, they are $2 each and the money goes to the foundation in James' name.

Please continue to pray for James, we are in need of them. The other day I was picking up some medicine and the lady in front of me was complaining about her kids. She looked at me and said, "If you don't have kids now, don't have them, they are trouble." I just smiled at her. She doesn't realize how lucky she is. I hope she does soon, we treasure every minute with James and Allison. Family and friends are wonderful and we need you; there really aren't any strangers anymore because so many have been touched by James. When they leave messages with us we see how this web (Caring Bridge) keeps evolving. We have met many on this journey and continue to pray and lift them up in their healing. The Lord is working miracles and we have one with our son. May God's blessings be with all of you. Until next time…

Praying for James,

Jim

SUNDAY, JANUARY 22, 2006 – 9:41 P. M.

"Without faith, it is impossible to please God, because anyone who comes to Him must believe that He exists and that He rewards those who earnestly seek Him." (Hebrews 11:6)

Faith is the one thing we can't do without. Faith is what will prevail on James' journey. We have days when things aren't going well, but they always turn around. Has to be Jesus, and faith.

James had a great weekend. He spent Friday night with a friend, we weren't sure how this would go, but when I saw him in the backseat with his friend, it was two buddies with the world in front of them. In fact, he was not ready to come home the next day, this hurt, but I loved it! He was being a little boy, even with a port and all he has been through. With his classmates he traveled to Children's Theater and had a great time. One day at a time, I guess. Today the two of us were running some errands and I could tell he was thinking about something. When I asked, he said, "Dad, I'm going to beat this cancer, because Jesus is in my heart. He's taking care of me." All I could do was smile and say, "You're right." He has experienced more and knows more than I ever will. He has been touched and this family is blessed. Tonight he wanted to spend the night with grandparents; they will get a dose of

Power Rangers, Disney and legos – what a life. Tomorrow he goes to Children's (hospital) for a photo shoot for a fundraiser.

Praying for James,

Jim

TUESDAY, JANUARY 24, 2006 – 3:33 P.M.

"Be still before the Lord and wait patiently for Him." (Psalm 37:7)

They say patience eliminates worry. It's tough not to sometimes; we have to keep believing. I know Jesus knows what we need better than we do, but we keep reminding Him. I don't think it hurts. I know He is preparing and strengthening us for our battle and if you want to know strong and tough, come see James.

The photo shoot was delayed; we are kicking back and waiting. James has adopted a favorite saying about his cancer, courtesy of a friend from Australia, via Caring-Bridge. Ask James and he says, "I'm going to kick that cancers butt out the window." He then will throw his head back and laugh. That confidence is heartwarming. It will all start with him; as long as he fights, we win. We are all in his corner. You can feel the prayers when we go out. When we picked Allison up today at school, at least 30 kids were yelling, "hey James!" He sat in the car and smiled. He has touched many and it is still growing.

He started another med today to help his appetite. He has eaten better today so maybe we are turning a corner. If not, the next step is to talk with a nutrionist. Looks like a day to day thing. Keep praying for our little boy. Please go hug your kids, parents, or someone you care about. You never know…

Praying for James,

Jim

MONDAY, JANUARY 30, 2006- 9:18 P.M.

"Commit your way to the Lord; trust in Him, and He will act." (Psalm 37:5)

We have, we are, and know He will.

We go to Children's Wednesday, clinic for a check-up, then to the all important MRI. He has three different chemos and spends the night. If all goes well after the many tests we go home on Thursday, please pray for good news. We are anxious, but we know who is in charge. Please, when you go to bed tomorrow night, say an extra prayer for James. We will.

Praying for James,

Jim

WEDNESDAY, FEBRUARY 1, 2006 – 11:29 P.M.

"This is my doing." (1 Kings 12:24)

No doubt about that. Praise His name, He gets all the glory. We realized at the beginning of this that our concerns and worries were His as well. We aren't here by accident, but right where Jesus wants us to be. He is leading us along a path and I'm so thankful that He has, and is holding our son's hand.

We are at Children's for our overnight treatment. The MRI showed nothing. No cancer, nothing in the tumor bed, no residual anywhere. The doctor said the only thing post op on the film was the scar on James' head. The nurse was right; the radiation folks were "great shots." That is what we have been praying for and it was answered. We are still in the beginning stages of this marathon, but we are off to a wonderful start. When his doctor examined him she said he looked awesome. It was wonderful to hear. We have such great admiration and respect for her and we trust her. Not because we have to, but we want to. She is tremendous. Angela and "Clay" came to see him as well. This wonderful lady always puts a smile on James' face. It started with the Lord giving Dr. Shativi such wonderful skill. Doc, looks like you didn't miss anything! His blood work looked great as well. James slept from noon – 4:30. He was pretty hungry when he woke up and that was great as well. We told him the cancer wasn't in his head any more and his response was, "You mean I kicked that cancer's butt out the window?" You sure did, little pal. He is on three chemos tonight. One was a shot in the "noodle." The second was oral, five capsules mixed with water in a syringe, and the last is a drip that will take about 6 hours to complete. They will weigh him when the bag is finished. They want to make sure his kidneys and liver are functioning before they release him. All his plumbing was working well when Allison and I left. Sherry is staying with him tonight. Please pray he doesn't throw up. We have a hearing test in the a.m. and after that, we hope it is home. We know he will be worn out, but tonight we are in the clouds.

Thanks to our families and friends, this could not be done without you. Friends have come together in prayer and James is proof of the answer. Thank you to our minister for the visit and prayers; we need his pipeline. Please continue the love and support for James. This is a new chapter, but through God's grace, James will meet the challenge.

Praying for James,

Jim

SATURDAY, FEBRUARY 4, 2006 – 9:56 A.M.

"Whatever you ask for in prayer, believe that you have received it, and it will be yours." (Mark 11:24)

James is proof of this. We continue to ask Jesus for help and He responds. He has given our son a better chance and we are blessed and thankful. We continue to ask for complete healing in James and we are confident this will happen. We will continue to believe.

James has been doing great since we returned home. His appetite isn't where it needs to be, but we keep offering choices. He hasn't shown any ill effects from the chemo and we pray this continues. He wakes up with a smile on his face and he keeps saying, "I kicked that cancer's butt out the window!" Thanks again Jay for his favorite saying! We are going to give school a shot next week. We have seen a change in James and we will try to ease him back in with his buddies. He tells us he misses them.

Please continue to pray for James. We know the power of prayer. James knows it is working. He continues to tell me that Jesus is in his heart and they walk together. How can you not feel great hearing that? We know, because we have seen that Jesus can take care of James better than us. That is what gets us through the day.

Praying for James,

Jim

MONDAY, FEBRUARY 6,, 2006 – 8:19 P.M.

"He knows the way that I take; when He has tested me, I will come forth as gold." (Job 23:10)

They say faith grows during storms. Faith is bringing the unseen into plain view. It makes the impossible seem possible. James has been there. We continue to follow where Jesus will lead.

James continues to amaze us. He has not been sick once from the chemo. Jesus is watching over him. He made it to school for a couple of hours this morning. He was fired up to see his buddies. He went in his room with a big smile on his face and one of his friends came up to him, rubbed his head and sat down to play – just being guys. We will try and ease him into a normal day, if we can remember what they are. He went to Grandma and DJ's for the afternoon and helped bake a cake, he is in a fabulous mood. We don't know what tomorrow will bring, but we will face it as a family. We go Wednesday for another chemo; he will have his port accessed as well. The good news is, it's just a visit and we go home after, no overnight.

At church Sunday our minister said, "Love isn't to be paid back, it's to be passed on." I see what my parents have always said, one day, you will understand about your kids. The love they have given us is to be passed on to mine. For now, we are thankful for each day with our kids. Please go and love on yours.

Praying for James,

Jim

WEDNESDAY, FEBRUARY 8, 2006 – 7:45 P.M.

"For by grace you have been saved through faith. And this is not our own doing; it is the gift of God." (Ephesians 2:8)

We have put our trust in Him. We know He will be with us no matter what. It was hard today for us. We saw people we knew today (at clinic) and they have a big battle as well. Our prayers are with them. We have no problems compared with others. Please count your blessings. The Lord blesses us everyday.

James did great; Dr. Reddy said he looked great and that he had a twinkle in his eye. She asked what he was eating; we said for the past 4-5 days it's been Doritos, ketchup and glasses of milk. She looked at me and said, "Milk is good…" She is always so positive. She put James through his paces and he was awesome.

Please continue the prayers for James. This hasn't ended. Prayers are being answered; there is no doubt about that. Please say some for all other kids at Children's (hospital) and their families as well. We are in much better shape that many others and for that we are thankful. Jesus has a plan for James and we will continue to follow faithfully. Thanks for your love.

Praying for James,

Jim

Sunday, February 12, 2006 – 6:36 p.m.

"Your heavenly Father knows." (Matthew 6:32)

I watch James sleeping at night. His breathing relaxes me and I find myself saying prayers over him. I'll put my hand on him and say a short one. I'll do this on and off 15 or 20 times, just talking with Jesus trying to find our path. I may ask for the same think over and over, sometimes I just don't know. I'm glad He knows what we need. I really believe that understanding will come one day. Not just for me, but for James, Allison, Sherry, grandparents and everyone who reads these words. Some days seem dark, but everything will take its proper place one day in God's great plan. I know it's one that will be so over-whelming and wonderful; we will all laugh with delight. He has big plans for our "little man."

Sherry said today that if James had hair you'd never know what was going on. James and I made it to church this morning and as we walked up for Communion James said hello to our minister. He looked at him and had a wonderfully warm smile on his face. You could see in his eyes the happiness James brings. I showed James what we did and although he didn't want the bread and wine, he did kneel with me and we said a prayer. He spoke with many today. It was a good day and we are thankful. We will go for our chemo on Wednesday and then, hopefully we will have 3 weeks off.

Please continue praying for our son. Eating is still an issue; his appetite comes and goes but it seems milk is the most nutritional on the list. Give your kids an extra hug tonight. I'm spending more time with Allison. As strong as she seems to be, she looks to us for assurance. God's love and joy to all or you.

Praying for James,

Jim

THURSDAY, FEBRUARY 16, 2006 – 7:32 P.M.

"My hope comes from Him." (Psalm 62:5)

We will continue to give God the credit for James. Faith is our opportunity to honor Him by the confidence we show. I was talking with someone today and she said the faith we were showing was great. I said we had turned this over to Him a long time ago and we know He is in control. That is the comfort.

James didn't have a very good morning. His head and stomach were hurting and his ears were ringing. All are side effects of the chemo. He had the last one yesterday. He is off for the next 3 weeks. We start the next round March 15. Sherry and I are checking our blood type. James is O-. Dr. Reddy said it wasn't a matter of if he would need blood, but when. Another hurdle we will meet with God's blessing. He was feeling better when I got home and we are about to watch a movie.

Thanks for your prayers. James was picked up on some other prayer lists locally and in California. Jesus is in control, no doubt. We are always praying for James.

In Christ,

Jim

SUNDAY, FEBRUARY 19, 2006 – 8:50 P.M.

"Give all your worries and cares to God, for He cares about what happens to you." (1 Peter 5:7)

I sure am glad He can handle this. We couldn't do it ourselves. The thing that is so comforting is Jesus cares and lets it show through the love of family and friends. We have been blessed with volunteers of blood donation for James. It has shown us how James has touched so many. The lord does work through prayer. I had forgotten my blood type and when my doctor called me with the news (I can give my blood to James) I gave thanks to the Lord above. I will let those wonderful people know if they are needed. Thank you doesn't seem like it will do, but like I've said before, thanks is what we have to give.

James had his first baseball practice Saturday morning in the gym at St. Marks. I wasn't sure if he would make it until I saw those beautiful eyes open and he asked, "Dad, are we playing baseball today?" He was a little shy at the beginning and his stamina was waning, but he pushed through. He walked over to Sherry twice and asked if he could go home, and both times she said, "Do you really want to leave?" He finished practice and the coach said he hit well and he smiled when he made it to first base. Hopefully it will be a great season.

At church this morning we prayed for tough love with James. We are taking Dr. Reddy's advice and will take things away from James unless he gives the effort to eat. Sherry had tears in her eyes this morning but the prayers have already been answered. James said mom was being mean, but she held her ground and he has had three yogurts this afternoon along with milk. One step and day at a time.

Thanks to all again for answering the blood call. I feel like a vampire, but the response is humbling. We couldn't do this alone and thankfully we aren't. Please pray for James as we are.

In Christ,

Jim

WEDNESDAY, FEBRUARY 22, 2006 – 8:30 P.M.

" ...Everything is possible for him who believes." (Mark 9:23)

Every time I look a passage fits James. We believe and we take Him at His word. We know He hears our prayers and that they are answered.

When I found out I was O- I looked up and gave thanks. James thinks it's cool that he will have my blood in him. If he only knew what we would do for him. What I wish I could take away from those eyes as they look at me. I pray daily that James will find some kind of peace that a 4 year old (5 on Monday) can have or take with him. We pray together and he asks that his cancer be taken from him. We tell him daily that there are so many people praying the same thing. We believe and we will fight.

Thanks to all who have volunteered to give blood. Prayers are answered yet again. I'm going tomorrow for the first round. My blood is good for 28 days after they "clean" it and a non-blood relative is good for 42 days. Sherry and I are checking the days and talking to the doctors to find out the best way to do this.

Give your kids a hug today and tell all that they are loved. Don't let a day go by.

In Christ,

Jim

SUNDAY, FEBRUARY 26, 2006 – 11:18 P.M.

"Dear friends, don't be surprised at the fiery trials you are going through, as if something strange were happening to you. Instead, be very glad—because these trials will make you partners with Christ in his suffering, and afterward you will have the wonderful joy of sharing His glory when it is displayed to the entire world." (1 Peter 4: 12-13)

It will be the start of James' 5th birthday in less than an hour. A year ago at this time we were looking at many, many more. Tomorrow we will give thanks that we have number 5. We aren't going to take anything for granted anymore. He is looking forward to a big day. Cupcakes with his school buddies in the morning, toy shopping in the afternoon and a party at home that night. To be five again! By the grace of God we will celebrate.

I took James to baseball practice Saturday morning at the gym. He had a lot of fun; the Cubs will dominate this year! This morning as we were headed to church, James told me about his dream from the night before. He said he was playing ball and hit it out the window of the gym. I think he is happy about baseball. Anything to be normal. His buddies are right there with him. He slept a little more this weekend and ate a little better. Hopefully we can make it to March 15 and not have to go to the hospital any sooner.

Please continue to pray for James. We give thanks to our Lord that we have had five wonderful years with him. Things aren't ideal, but there are many people out there with more challenges than us. We pray for them. I've thanked my Savior for allowing me to have him for 5 wonderful years. One day we will look back on this and smile. Jesus has a plan for our "little man."

Praying for James,

Jim

THURSDAY, MARCH 2, 2006 – 9:22 P.M.

"You do not realize now what I am doing, but later you will understand." (John 13:7)

We sure don't, not in this life anyway, but one day we will see what Jesus has in store for James and our family. His plans aren't finished, but one day we will laugh and understand.

James had a great birthday. It's been more like a birthday week! Monday it was family, friends, presents and Spiderman cake. He was worn out that night. Tuesday he was at the Rebel baseball game and was on the field with Coach Davis and the players for the team prayer. He thought it was cool to be on the field with the "big boys." Later at home, Allison was eating a burger and fries. He thought the fries smelled good and ended up eating them all. I went to B-yard Burger and bought 2 more of the "straight fires" (as James calls them) and he ate them for breakfast. These were his first fries in two months! Wednesday night he had baseball practice and thoroughly enjoyed himself. He hit well, took a ground ball off his chest, stayed with it and made the throw to first. After practice we bought 3 packs of curly fries and they were polished off. Drinkable yogurts, milk, Fritos and fries for now. He went to the zoo today with his school buddies. He rode the train and his buds waited on him at the monkey house. They yelled for him to play and he ran to them. We are trying to get some normalcy in our lives. His tastes and maybe the desire for some foods are coming back. Another prayer answered. Sometimes we forget that He answers the small ones as well as the big.

We are thankful for another day with James. His will is strong and the body is trying to keep up. We pray for his strength and healing daily and we feel the prayers that are said for James. We are in this fight and aren't letting up. God's grace will see to James' needs. We are blessed to have such wonderful family and friends. The support is generous. Love on your kids tonight. They deserve it. Make sure you tell someone you love them as well. You never know what tomorrow brings.

Praying for James,

Jim

MONDAY, MARCH 6, 2006 – 7:30 P.M.

"Summon your power, O God; show us your strength." (Psalm 68:28)

There is no doubt that we are drawing all our strength from the Lord. He has and will continue to give James the strength to get through this. We have been shown this

asking all weekend about it. I love hearing him look forward to things. He wants to go to school tomorrow and see his friends; he is awesome. You never know what he is going to say or remember, he is awesome.

Please keep James in your prayers; he needs them. We will continue our prayer list. If you can add him to another one, please do. Please remember the kids at Childrens' Hospital. We know we are blessed, God is watching over our son.

Praying for James,

Jim

SATURDAY, APRIL 1, 2006 – 6:08 P.M.

"Consider what God has done: Who can straighten what He has made crooked?" (Ecclesiastes 7:13)

Although it seems we have found ourselves in a place where escape is going to be tough, we are finding the circumstances we face are being led by Him and He will guide us. We are in a very serious situation and we trust what we don't understand. Although there are times we are filled with uncertainty, we know Jesus is going to display His grace and power and not only deliver us, but teach us a lesson we will never forget. We know when this happens we will never be able to thank Him enough for what He is doing for us now.

Last week was very busy; James was in clinic on Wednesday for treatment. His doctor said he looked great and he did not need any blood. Unless he gets a fever she does not need to see him until April 26. We will do our best to make that happen.

This brings me to something we need to address. James' school has been great to stay up on this and it's something we've never thought about, until James started his cancer battle. Please, if anyone that is around or going to be around James is sick or gets sick, please call us day or night – 24/7. He is very prone to any illness with his blood count being down and we have been keeping up with friends that are in the same battle as us. Infections, not just the cancer, have been the cause of many of our hospital friends having extended stays. Although we have been lucky, something like the chicken pox or as simple as a cold virus would be devastating for James. We lost a friend last week from infection; once it started it couldn't be controlled. We are going to miss this little friend but God will bless her family and He will welcome her with open arms. We will do our best to "keep him in a bubble" but we need everyone else as well. James is doing great with his battle and we would hate to see something as simple as a cold bring him down. We can't thank you enough for the support.   I was so proud of James today. We had a baseball game at noon and even though we had chemo 3 days ago he made the game. He was running on fumes at the end but he was there. He had 3 hits and the Cubs prevailed in a close one! James' coach, teammates and their parents have been great. They understand that James is giving it his all.

The problem we are having with this round of chemo is he is hungry, but we can't seem to find much he will eat. He shows interest, but only snacks.

We continue to pray for our extended family that battle everyday with the same things as us. By God's grace, He will lift us up. We will all see His plan one day and we will understand. Until then, we will continue this fight.

Praying for James,

Jim

MONDAY,, APRIL 10, 2006 – 9:30 P.M.

"Don't worry about anything; instead, pray about everything. Tell God what you need, and thank Him for all He has done. If you do this, you will experience God's peace, which is far more wonderful than the human mind can understand. His peace will guard your hearts and minds as you live in Christ Jesus." (Philippians 4:6-7)

Being parents it is hard not to worry, but not believing in Christ is not an option. His grace is seen each and every day with James. I've said this before, one day we will understand and we will smile when His glory is revealed. His love will show us where we need to be. We thank God each day we have together. Please do the same with our families.

James had an up and down week. Tuesday he came down with a stomach bug. The doctors said it was not chemo related, so we had to ride it out. He has lost weight that he could not afford and we are struggling to replace it. He is hungry and he tries, food just has a different taste. James' spirit is good, he went to his sister's dance recital where she performed her solo; he is her biggest fan. She is a ray of sunshine that we need. Tonight my heart warmed. Angel (our dog) went crazy running around the room. When she would fly by James he would start laughing. He couldn't catch his breath and tears were coming out of his eyes. He hasn't laughed like that in a long time. I can't tell you how wonderful it was to witness. Once again, the little things mean a lot. He has been on the deck playing basketball for the past couple of days. Great sign for us – we take what we can get.

Thank you for keeping James in your prayers. He continues to need them. We also ask that you keep a little girl named Leslie in your prayers. She is in ours. Mary or Mike, if you need us, please email us, or call. You are not alone. I urge you to turn this over to Christ. He is the ultimate doctor.

Praying for James,

Jim

WEDNESDAY, APRIL 12, 2006 – 10:30 P.M.

"What is faith?" It is the confident assurance that what we hope for is going to happen. It is the evidence of things we cannot yet see." (Hebrews 11:1)

We have faith. We certainly do not know what is going to happen, and it isn't in our hands. I know Jesus can take better care of James than me. It is hard sometimes, guess that's what makes us human. Although we can't see where we are going, we know Jesus will light our path.

James is eating a little better. Last night we met at Roly Poly and James ate a little, we left early and later when Sherry got home she said that the manager came up to her and said he wanted to donate some of the wraps to James.

(James only ate the wrap, not what was inside). James is touching people in ways I will never know.

James says he is ready for his game (baseball) tomorrow, said he is going to hit and field. What a ball player!

We got some tough news tonight from one of our very best friends, Andrew. He has been out of treatment for 6 months and went in yesterday for an MRI. The cancer was back in his brain and also they found it on his spine. The family is looking for options. We have a heavy heart and are praying for them. It is hitting home with us especially because of the similarities between James and him, and the treatments. This is where the faith comes in and where we are tested. I can't explain how we feel. Right now, our prayers are with this family. Please visit their Caringbridge page and lift them up.

Praying for James,

Jim

Saturday, April 15, 2006 – 7:41 p.m.

"Your Father knows exactly what you need even before you ask him." (Matthew 6:8)

I'm thankful He knows. It's much easier when He is in charge. This is a wonderful time of year. He is risen!

James had a good Friday practice and the game today was great. Even though it was hot, he was out there the whole time. He ran out of gas the last inning, but he was there, we are so proud of him. It hurts watching what this cancer, radiation and chemo have done to his body, but we will get strong again. Next year this time it will be a different story. He wants to go to church tomorrow which is a great sign; it shows me he is getting a little stronger. We have discovered cheese toast and he just polished some off and we are going to head to the ball park to see some of Allison's friends play.

Please pray for our friends; they have not made a decision on what course of treatment, pray for the parents to have the strength they need.

Happy Easter to everyone!

Praying for James,

Jim

Wednesday, April 19, 2006 – 9:32 p.m.

"The prayer given in faith will heal the sick man, and the Lord will raise him up." (James 5:15)

We are constantly praying for James. I can't tell you the number of times day and night they flow. You can feel them, it is wonderful. He is feeling pretty good. His bout with the stomach bug had us concerned and we can't get weight on him. He is active and burns it off; it is a catch 22. He laughed so hard at Angel (our Bichon dog) he lost his breath. It is wonderful to see him smile. He loves being on the deck and kicking the ball and playing basketball. He can't wait for his baseball practice and game later in the week.

Thank you for all of the prayers and thoughts. We read Caringbridge to James and if you could only see the smile. He is my hero. He teaches me every day and I love him more every day. We aren't sure if he will need blood yet but I'm giving tomorrow. If we need others, we will be in touch, thank you all for the offer. Thanks also to those who let us know when James may have been exposed to some type of sickness. I may get redundant, but we really need to know if he is around anyone who may have been ill. He just isn't able to bounce back and I never knew the importance of knowing until now.

Praying for James,

Jim

SUNDAY, APRIL 23, 2006 – 9:08 P.M.

"The Lord will work out his plans for my life—for your faithful love, O Lord, endures forever. Don't abandon me, for you made me." (Psalm 138:8)

We know He will not leave us. One day we will understand. It is very hard. We have many sleepless nights. I was having one of those last night, when I felt James' breath against my hand. I felt all of the burden leave and once again, I knew who was in control.

James has had a pretty good weekend. For some reason, there have been mountains and valleys. He is full of energy one minute and has none the next. Friday night we were bachelors. We went to the Relay for Life at the high school. They asked me if I would tell James' story. The students were great. I've never been a public speaker, but if it will raise money to find a cure for this evil disease, I will do anything.

We were not sure if we would make baseball on Saturday, it had rained all night and James was not feeling very well Saturday morning. We made the game; he would bat, but needed a runner. He played 2 innings in the field. After the game the coach picks someone to go to the mound and call everyone else around. James did it. The kids do a "Go cubs" by themselves. It's great. James took a 3 hour nap when we got home.

Next Tuesday we will spend 2 nights for treatment; we are praying for this treatment to be as quick and painless as the others. These are new chemos, so we aren't sure what will happen. Please pray for no side effects.

Praying for James,

Jim

TUESDAY, APRIL 25, 2006 – 11:29 P.M.

"Everyone who calls on the name of the Lord will be saved." (Joel 2:32)

We find out how blessed we are when we go to Children's (Hospital). We are in much better shape considering… I don't know where this path is leading us, but I do trust Him. He isn't asking for my help or advice, but I know if we will follow and believe, He will deliver us. This is a given.

It's been a long day for James; he is so tough. He didn't flinch when they did his port. He said he was going to do what Dr. Reddy asked so we could get to the room and get the chemo over with. He is my hero. Dr. Reddy said he looked "awesome," and he did not need any blood. Another prayer answered. Her smile told us all we needed. Good news sometimes seems lost when you are in clinic. We are very blessed to have her as our doctor. We made it to the hospital room and then it was hooking up the fluids and chemo. It hurts knowing the poison is going into your son's body. We just pray it is doing its job and not giving any of the bad side effects. James drank several milks and yogurts and ate Doritos and pretzels. I hope that trend continues. God love him, he was worried more about his sister tonight than himself. He wanted me to make sure she and Angel got some "good sleep." Little buddy, I pray you do as well. His face lit up when Allison got to his room; he wanted to show her the 100 piece puzzle he did by himself. Spiderman, who would've guessed?

Please consider supporting the "Wheeling-for-Hope" fundraiser, there is a website. It gives us a stronger conviction to find a cure when we are in clinic. So many children, it will break you heart. We plan on fighting for the rest of our time on this earth to find a cure. Thank all of you for the prayers and support. We tell James the number of people that are praying for him and he flashes his smile; it's great to see. He keeps saying that Jesus is in his heart. He knows more than we do. God bless him and all of you.

Praying for James,

Jim

WEDNESDAY, APRIL 26, 2006 – 11:01 P.M.

"For when I am weak, I am strong." (2 Corin. 12:10)

This is what we have to remember, when we are at our lowest, all we have to do is call on His strength. He is in control. Thank goodness!

Dorothy was right, there is no place like home. We made it around 9:45 p.m. We didn't care, James is sleeping in his bed tonight and the only sounds are ours. Sherry will probably get up during the night and open the door to let a nurse in! James still doesn't understand why they keep waking him up. Same here buddy; just let a man sleep. His sodium was down this morning, but around 2:00 Richard said they were perfect. We had our 2nd chemo this afternoon; this cycle was rougher than the first 2 round. James had to have some nausea meds to calm his tummy down. This knocked him out and he slept most of the afternoon. To me, it's not a tough call. I would rather him sleep and not eat than be awake and sick and not eating. The good news is he is hungry when he wakes up. He just ate some Johnny Rays chocolate pie, Doritos, pretzels and milk. The light is off and he and Angel are snuggled up together. Angel went crazy when he got home and that made James feel good. We have to watch a number of things for the next 48 hours. This one has different side effects. Fever is one of them, so James is now in the bubble.

Time for the lights to go out here. Thank you Jesus for another day. Thank you for picking us up when we are down; we can always count on You.

Praying for James,

Jim

Sunday, April 30, 2006 – 10:14 p.m.

"Your faithfulness extends to every generation, as enduring as the earth you created. Your laws remain true today, for everything serves your plans." (Psalms 119:90-91)

We have faith that Christ is in control. We are serving him, and thank him everyday for everything. I've said that James is in a win, win. Jesus doesn't need our advice. He has this.

This has been a week of ups and downs for James. His moods change with the wind. I hate the chemo. I wish it would just do its job and give none of the side effects. He slept a lot on Friday. Saturday morning Allison and I ran at the Dogwood Run. James was there to cheer Allison on; he feels pretty good in the morning and runs out of steam in the early afternoon. After the run he and Allison took Angel to the "dog parade." James was in heaven with all of the dogs around. He had every intention of making his baseball game at 12:30 but around 11:00 he wanted to take a rest and he slept until 3:30. He wants to make the baseball party on Friday at the Barons Game. Time will tell. I'm proud of him for just wanting to go to the game. He has to take long rests in the afternoons. The chemo is working him over. It's tough to watch, but God has his plan.

Thanks to everyone for the support and prayers. We can't do this alone, and we can feel all of the love. Please hug your kids tonight and maybe look the other way on some of the things they may do. We have some other friends we are praying for who have some very tough times ahead. They are not alone. Christ is with them as He is with us. For that, we are blessed.

Praying for James,

Jim

WEDNESDAY, MAY 3 – 9:17 P.M.

"For it is God who works in you to will and to act according to His good purpose." (Philippians 2:13)

James is affecting people we know and those we will never know. He is my inspiration and hero. Christ is using James to make a difference. One day we will understand why.

We are a third of the way in our chemos; 6 cycles left. James continues to amaze us and the doctors. Dr. Reddy used the "awesome" word again. James was talkative and she was smiling as she listened. He has been feeling pretty good the last few days. It warms my heart to see his smile and hear his laughter. The only bad thing today for James (at clinic) was his white blood count; it was low. Dr. Reddy wasn't overly concerned, but she cautioned us to keep him close to home and limit his contact. He won't be going to school the rest of the week. We can't risk him being around any type of sickness. We have come too far to let something as simple as a cold knock him down. Looks like lots of hand washing and face wiping. Thanks to everyone for understanding. I'm glad he made it to the zoo yesterday with his friend, Lindsey. Sherry called me when they were eating pizza. I could hear the laughter as I raised the phone; I had tears in my eyes. It was great to hear him. James really liked seeing the snakes at the zoo – I have no idea where that comes from! Last night he talked about the zoo in his sleep. Some friends need James for a photo for a fundraiser, but it's on hold until next week as we try to get his counts up. He did gain a half pound since last week.

I got some tough news this afternoon. A high school friend, Benny, has learned he has cancer. Please put him on any prayer list you can. Pray for him, his wife and their 3 beautiful daughters. I saw him today and his attitude is great. He is in the best town and he knows it. His faith is there and that is what will get him through this. He and his brother have been very generous to us in our fundraisers for cancer. We don't understand the reasons on this earth, but one day, it will be revealed. They will be in our prayers.

We lost another brave little "super hero" yesterday. Kadin has his angel wings and is dancing with Cassidy. You can hear the laughter in heaven. No more ouches; God bless them and their wonderful families.

This has been a hard entry for me. No one is promised anything, so please love on your kids. Please don't take one second for granted and live each day as if it were your last. I'm sitting here typing and James and I are carrying on a conversation with a movie going. He just told me, "Dad, I love you and I like you." You too pal, you too.

Praying for James,

Jim

MONDAY, MAY 8, 2006 – 10:22 P.M.

"One day Jesus told his disciples a story to illustrate their need for constant prayer and to show them that they must never give up." (Luke 18:1)

We have to remember that this isn't over. James is doing well, but we have to keep praying. James isn't quitting and neither are we. We have to pray until what we want is accomplished, or we have complete assurance in our hearts that it will be. The worst thing we can do is stop the prayers. We aren't giving in.

Tonight James couldn't find his blanket to go to sleep with. He told Sherry, "I hope Daddy finds my blanket because I want to take it to heaven with me." That hit hard. We asked about it and he said he had a dream the other night that he was in heaven with 2 angels; a little boy and girl. He said they were playing with their parents on a swing. He told Sherry he would miss her when he goes to heaven. What do you say to that? We told him not to be scared, but we are. We weren't expecting this to come out of his mouth tonight. We were about to go to bed, but sleep is going to be hard for me tonight. It was like he was preparing us, but we can't go there. This is what is hard to comprehend on this earth. Christ has this laid out; we just can't see it yet. I say that one day we will understand. Sometimes it's easier to say. James is sleeping so well now, but I don't think Sherry and I will let go of him tonight, or sleep. I find myself listening to him and taking everything that I can in. It's hard to put these feelings down. Just when I feel the pressure and the thoughts zinging through my head, I hear him and I get a peace around me. I want so badly for Sherry to find this, but I don't have the answers. This is why we still need every prayer we can get. Sorry for the ramble, but this helps me. Right now Sherry is asleep by him and I find comfort with that.

We go in the morning to check his white count. This is the first time we have done this and it is frightening. Even though we have come a long way, we still have a lot to go. It's a marathon and a tough one.

Please remember to pray for our friends who are also fighting this disease. One friend is in Houston for treatment and another opinion. We aren't alone in this, this evil affects many. We have to find a cure and do it now. I don't want anymore of this for anyone.

Praying for James,

Jim

TUESDAY, MAY 9, 2006 – 9:36 P.M.

"What can I offer the Lord for all he has done for me?" (Psalm 116.12)

Our faith. He knows what we cry out for, He knows what we need. We just have to continue our course and believe.

Last night was tough on us. James threw us for a loop with his dream. He has a vision I will never know and has experienced things we hope to one day understand. That day will be a glorious one indeed. We made it to clinic and checked our blood. It was what we thought, not much change. Whites were down and his reds were ok. No blood need, yet. Dr. Reddy said it was amazing that he didn't need blood because he is so pale. We go back Friday and check again. Sherry and I needed to see Dr. Reddy today. James has been having some headaches and double vision and we were worried. She said it was his low white count. Never thought I would be happy with an anemic son, but from what Sherry and I were thinking, it was good news. She said the chemo from his last hospital stay knocked him around. No doubt about that. Sherry told her about his dream and Dr. Reddy had to sit in a chair. You could see her tear up and she said that James was telling us he was going to be alright. She said James was going to get through this and that he would be fine. We agreed one way or another he would be. We needed her words today. I can't tell you how we needed them; she is very special to us. We told her we visited Andrew (our dear friend) during a lull in the blood work. He was about to go home (from Children's) after about a week in the hospital. Andrew and James were talking and laughing and it seemed like there were five conversations going on at once. Andrew felt and looked good and Dr. Reddy was very pleased to hear about our visit. She said when James would need to come back on Friday to check his blood again. She didn't want to give him a shot to boost his white count, not yet anyway. He may have to have blood as well; we will wait and see. She said he could make his baseball game Saturday, providing he felt ok. She also said he could go to Allison's recital Saturday afternoon. James is looking forward to seeing her dance. He also wants to watch his "Strawberry Shortcake Lindsey" and "Dalmatian Hannah" dance their cute little hearts and booties off! We jut have to watch him close. Any fever and we would be in the hospital for several days.

Thanks to all of our family and friends for the thoughts and prayers. We need them now more than ever. We are taking this slow and then we slow down more. I want this nightmare to end, but it's ours to endure. Thanks to all for being behind us. Thank you for praying and loving my son and family.

Praying for James,

Jim

SATURDAY, MAY 13, 2006 – 9:21 P.M.

"I asked the Lord to give me this child, and he has given me my request. Now I am giving him to the Lord, and he will belong to the Lord his whole life." (I Samuel 1:27)

He was given to Jesus long ago. We are blessed every minute of every day that we have James. He is one awesome "little man." Jesus has this, and is in control. A friend told me yesterday that God doesn't make mistakes; everything is going exactly as He has planned. James told me not to worry as well. James walked with Jesus again two nights ago. In this flesh it hurts to hear his dreams, but in my heart, I know James has the ultimate doctor and protector. I sure don't have the answers, but He does, and I am thankful for that.

Our Friday visit for blood work showed James with better white counts. They were better that Wednesday, but not great. He did not need blood (transfusion) and that was good. He is eating a little better and hopefully they will continue to rise. When we said our prayers Friday night, He asked Jesus to let him be able to play in his last baseball game of the season and go to Allison's dance recital. Both were answered. Dr. Reddy said he could go with precautions. The game wasn't her concern, but dance was. James left everything he had on the field. We were the home team and he played 3 innings in the field and in the 3rd he played first and caught a ball for an out. The smile said it all. In his last at bat for the season he got a hit and made it to first. He looked at me and said, "Dad, I'm too tired to run the bases again." I had to carry him to the dugout. He was smiling as everyone cheered and I had a tear in my eye. He is the bravest and toughest person I know. He is my hero. After the game the coach presented him with his trophy. (We had missed the team party earlier because of chemo). Once again, his smile said it all. The coach also gave James a certificate that was for the "player of the year." James had a great year. I can't tell you how proud we are of him. He missed 2 games from this awful stuff and never complained. James is the man! Dr. Reddy said he could to the recital if he wore a mask. He did, with no complaints. I wore one as well and we found seats away from everyone. We were in the balcony, but down the side in a single seat; he could see everything. Allison was wonderful and James was her biggest cheerleader. I do not know where Allison gets the stage presence, and whatever "it" is, she has. James was happy to watch Lindsey and Hannah and he cheered for both. He was picking out Allison's friends and clapping. Anna, Devin, Leah, Lauren and many others. They were all great. Allison's solo was fabulous. She is great for James, in so many ways. Sherry and I are truly blessed. Granma and DJ are so proud of both of them, and don't miss an opportunity to be at their functions. We are blessed to have them as well. James and I made it home and he took a 2 hour nap. Listening to him breathe relaxes me and puts the world into perspective. Angel was by him the entire time. She is a great doggie for him. He is watching the Wizard of Oz because of Allison dancing to "The Wiz" in her first number. You never know what kids are thinking. They are a gift from God. Thanks to our friends for all the meals. Sherry and I were feeling a little guilty because James feels pretty good, but maybe that is why. We are spending out time caring for him and Allison and the meals give us the freedom to use that time for them. He ate a little pizza tonight, but the yogurts and milk are the key. Please continue to pray for James. He doesn't go back to the hospital until May 23. We have an overhaul then. MRI, hearing tests, the works. Scary, but part of the process. Please start praying that the MRI is as clear as the one in February.

Please keep Andrew and his family in your prayers as well; he made it to his class party Friday – great news – give him a shout!

Please pray for Benny as well. There are a lot of people that need our prayers. Thanks to all of you and to all you Moms out there, Happy Mothers Day!

Praying for James,

Jim

THURSDAY, MAY 18, 2006 – 10:27 P.M.

"Pour out thy heart like water before the face of the Lord: Lift up thy hands toward Him for the life o thy young children." (Lamentations 2:19)

We have done this. I can't count the breakdowns we've had. But by the grace of God, we keep going and James keeps fighting. He is so strong; he knows his limits. One minute he is playing his heart out and then he rests. He gains some strength and he is off again. That strength is from Jesus, no doubt. James has had a pretty good week. We can tell his counts are not where they need to be, but he has not had a fever. We count our blessings for that. He was able to go to Hannah's birthday party today. He had talked about it all week, so there was nothing that would or could hold him back. He liked watching Hannah open her presents and like all wild 5 year old parties he came back with a snake tattoo. Crazy kids. James is fired up for DoDah Day that is Saturday. Last night he was just about asleep and the commercial came on TV advertising the festivities and he sat straight up in bed smiling. All of those dogs and so little time. He is also ready for Sunday and the "Wheeling for Hope." Please join if you can. I think he just wants to be involved with everything. His little mind is so sharp. He reminds us of things we need to be doing. The past 3 days have found us playing ball in the afternoon. His hitting is coming along. I soft toss to him and he is hitting up the middle. He does enjoy this and I treasure the moments.

We go back Tuesday for the MRI. The waiting is the worst. You put it in the back of your mind, but it is always around. Please pray for the same result from February. God is watching over James and He doesn't make mistakes. Thanks to everyone who prays for James; you can feel them. Thanks for the wonderful meals as well. You think you have time in the evening to cook and something seems to come up. They are welcomed. Please keep

Andrew, Leslie, JJ, Davis, Scarlett and Benny in your prayers. They are all so special.

Praying for James,

Jim

SUNDAY, MAY 21, 2006 – 10:33 P.M.

"For I know the plans I have for you declares the Lord, plans to prosper you and not to harm you, plans to give you hope and a future." (Jeremiah 29:11)

Hope and future. That is what we pray for. Wheeling for Hope (fundraiser) was a great start. Maybe the money raised today will one day find a cure for this awful, awful disease. If one family doesn't have to experience what we have, it will be worth it. It was a great turnout for the bike ride. Looks like a great future for the event. It was great to see family and friends show up. Thanks to everyone. It means a lot when you have such wonderful support. James got to see Andrew today and my heart warms when I see them together. We saw a family that had recently lost their child to cancer and my heart goes out to them. It took a lot of faith and strength for them to be there, but it is something dear to their hearts, obviously. God bless them.

Please continue James in your prayers. We go in Tuesday for the MRI and chemos. Please pray for great results. We don't do this without support and thanks be to God for delivering. I had tears in my eyes when I saw so many smiling faces; James was able to ride his bike for a short time on the course and Allison and her buddies made the loop several times. This event has much potential and we will support it with all our heart and soul. Thanks to the organizers and volunteers for making this a success.

Praying for James,

Jim

MONDAY, MAY 22, 1006 – 10:01 P.M.

"As for God, his way is perfect; the word of the Lord is flawless. He is a shield for all who take refuge in Him." (II Samuel 22:31)

We are blessed because of this. His way is the only way. We know He doesn't make mistakes and although we don't understand the reasons on this earth, one day in Heaven, it will be clear. James is being protected by Him. My family as well. Thank you Jesus.

James is in great spirits. This is the tough part. He feels great, and we have to hit the hospital for more chemo. He had a great day at Granmas; they made cookies and planted flowers. We came home and got Allison and headed to the basketball court to play some baseball. He is hitting well. I hope he keeps that love for the game. We headed out to buy birthday stuff for Allison and James promised not to give any secrets away. He said, "Dad, I am a great secret-keeper." I have no doubt about that buddy. Sherry and I decided to have the MRI tomorrow instead of Wednesday. We wanted Allison's birthday to be as normal as possible, and hopefully, we will be home after we spend the night at the hospital. We are planning on an uneventful trip. With God leading the way, this will happen. Please pray for a clear MRI, great hearing test and no complications with the chemo. We need good blood counts and no fever or any other sickness. It's a lot to ask for, but that is what we want. Please pray for James to keep his appetite going and for staying strong. He told me he would never quit and I told him that we would never quit on him. He is my hero and I love that littleman with ever fiber of my being. He is awesome. He has taught me more about life and has taught me to pray better. God is working through him and He is bringing this family closer than ever. Jesus has a plan for James, but I'm too dense to see it. One day... one day. All we can do is keep giving God the glory and let him work. Wheeling for Hope showed Sherry and me what James is doing in other peoples lives. He has touched many, and will continue to do so. Please keep Andrew, Benny, JJ and Leslie in your prayers. Thank you Jesus for my family. Thanks for showing us your love through all of our family and our friends. You make no mistakes.

Praying for James,

Jim

TUESDAY, MAY 23, 2006 – 10:10 P.M.

"But Jesus called the children to Him and said, "Let the little children come to me, and do not hinder them, for the kingdom of God belongs to such as these." (Luke 18:16)

Praise Jesus! He is watching over our son. The MRI was clear. Dr. Reddy said everything looked great. His white and red counts were up, his hearing was good. It was a great visit, and we give our thanks and praise to Jesus. He is the ultimate healer. Tonight will be quick,

James is doing well. When he was going in for the MRI, James said something. Dorothy, the nurse, looked at Sherry and asked if she heard him right. Sherry said yes. James had asked, "Why are all of these angels flying around my head?" He is being protected. We are blessed. Allison asked her teacher if they could say a prayer this afternoon (at school) during his MRI. When she told me this tonight I cried. Allison is amazing and so loves her brother. God listens to the prayers of children. Thank you everyone for each and every prayer. Please keep them going for James and all of his friends at Children's. God bless you as well Benny

Praying for James,

Jim

SATURDAY, MAY 27, 2006 – 10:07 P.M.

"The Lord is good unto them that wait…" (Lamentations 3:25)

As bad as we want this marathon to end, we have to wait. I've said I want Christmas decorations up at Children's, that way I know we are close.

James has felt better this round than any other. His only problem was Thursday and that wasn't bad. His appetite isn't where we would like, but that happens after every treatment. He has been swimming the last couple of days and it is great to see. His attitude is great and he seems to have energy. It kind of goes up and down, but overall, he is doing well. Richard (at Clinic 8) told us the cycles will slowly start wearing him down. Evidently the chemo is building up, but James is strong, and we know

God will watch over him. It was like he was preparing us, but we will tackle those cycles as they come. Allison is with Devon at the lake for the weekend. As bad as we want to hold her close, we can't penalize her. We know she is in good hands, but that doesn't stop us from missing her. James has his friend, Noah, spending the night. We went to see "Over the Hedge" and the laughter from the two of them was wonderful to hear. Spiderman is on and the lights are off. Sleep tight guys.

Thank you all for the prayers and thoughts. They are working. Please continue them. Please visit Andrew's web page and keep him in your prayers. There is a special prayer service at the church next Wednesday. Go to his site for the update.

I talked to Benny on Friday and he was tired. I told him to stay strong; it will help with his girls and wife visiting. Please pray for him and all of the others we keep close to our hearts. Tell your kids that you love them and give them as many hugs as you can. Don't put anything that you want to say to someone off. Tell them now. Thank you for checking on James. His smile lights up the room when we read him the guestbook (of Carenbridge). We are going to enjoy the extra day off.

Praying for James,

Jim

SUNDAY, JUNE 4, 2006 – 10:25 P.M.

"The eyes of the Lord range throughout the earth to strengthen those whose hearts are fully committed to Him." (2 Chronicles 16:9)

We are a blessed family. James has been feeling pretty good all week. We know that there is no limit to what God can do, provided we don't seek the glory, but give it all to Him. James' appetite is good. Yogurts and milk are the mainstays. I left Allison and James on the computer earlier and our house sounded normal for the first time in months. I sat at the bottom of the stairs and listened…it was wonderful. Thank you Jesus. Please keep James in your prayers and thoughts.

Praying for James,

Jim

TUESDAY, JUNE 6, 2006 – 10:15 P.M.

"No eye has seen, no ear has heard, no mind has conceived that God has prepared for those who love Him, but God has revealed it to us by his Spirit." (1 Corinthians 2:9-10)

We know that God has a future that we can't even imagine. He sees what is impossible for us. I'm glad.

James asks what heaven is like and I tell him to think of his best day and then I say, "It is better than that." He smiles. He has been feeling good this week. He knows we go in tomorrow to check blood and get our chemo. He also knows we get 3 plus weeks off after. That makes him smile as well. Yesterday at work, my boss, Steve gave me a package that his 3 boys and wife ordered. It contained a fake roach, retractable money on a string, squirting nickel, pig nose and no start toilet paper. We had a good hour to set up to "trick" James' sister and mom. He put the roach in Allison's bed; the toilet paper in the bathroom, I filled the nickel, put the pig nose under his mom's pillow and when he heard the garage door go up, he hid under the table with the chair for cover and waited with the money on the string. What do you know, all of his tricks worked! He was laughing so hard he had tears. The roach worked 3 times on mom alone. The nickel worked best on Angel (our beloved dog). It was great to hear the laughter. Thanks to some other friends James got a "CARS" race-track from his chemo-angel Mary. He wrecked me for the better part of an hour. Angel Bobbi sent Allison a birthday gift. They are so special and James looks forward to the mail. Bobbi, if you get this, let us know how we can get in tough with you, we would love to see you when you make your trip through Tenn. and Alabama. James wants to see who you are. Be safe.

James and I have gotten into the habit of watching the sun set. We walk Angel and we watch the sun do down. Once again, it's the little things that mean so much. Please don't take a minute of being with your kids for granted. We cherish every day. My Aunt JoAnn in New Orleans has a friend in the Catholic Church that has the Priest doing his evening service for James and Andrew. Last night, special prayers were said for Andrew and tonight, they were said for James. The love shown is over-whelming and humbling. Sherry and I can't thank you enough. We are blessed. Please pray for good blood work and no complications from chemo. God bless all of you.

Praying for James,

Jim

SATURDAY, JUNE 10, 2006 – 2:43 P.M.

"…God has said, "Never will I leave you; never will I forsake you. "So we say with confidence, "The Lord is my helper; I will not be afraid. What can man do to me?" (Hebrews 13:5-6)

He is working through all of the doctors, nurses, family and loving friends for James. James is a very blessed little boy. We tell him about all of the people praying for him and he says he knows why. He says, "Dad is it because they love me?" You bet they do little pal. Jesus is in his heart, and we are thankful He is in control.

James had to get blood Thursday for the first time. He wasn't fazed in the least. Dr. Reddy and the staff were amazed he hasn't needed it sooner. It was just a matter of time. It brings out a whole new arena for us. We have to watch his red and white counts, and his platelets. We told him he would feel better. I carried him to the car afterwards and he said, "I don't feel like a new boy." You will buddy, you will. We have to watch out for infection, hives and any other reactions for the next few days. He was feeling good that afternoon. He was feeling good that afternoon; Granma and DJ came by in the early evening. I asked if he was hungry and he said he wanted to go to Diplomat Deli for a PB&J. You could have heard a pin drop in the room. He hasn't wanted that in months. Allison wanted to walk so Granma, DJ and James headed out. Sherry and I met them there and he ordered one with strawberry and grape jelly. We didn't say anything. When he started eating it we held our breath. He ate half, had a quart of milk, a cupcake and yogurt; it was great. We stopped by the basketball court on the way home and played baseball. Looks like the blood worked. Friday night found us at El Pob. Ms Nan and her crew brought Allison birthday stuff and James presents as well. They do love this little boy and we can't thank them enough. Nan is the one who gave us "Walter the Dog" and his books. If you don't know about "Walter," he has stomach problems. James loves it. We got a bonus and had his cousin Jaclyn eat dinner and spend the night with us. Laughter filled this house again. We played ball again last night and watched our sunset. James had a chocolate chip pancake with his sis and Jaclyn this morning. The appetite is a joy to see. God is watching over this home. We had an offer for the beach this next week, but we are going to give James some healing time. Friends were great to think of us and we will go next time. James is still a little up and down and we are still watching his white counts. We are off from treatments until July 12, so we are planning some fun. We will just take it slow. We only go back if he gets a fever. Please pray for no complications on anything.

Thanks to all who check in on James. He has touched many and God is smiling. He is using James in a very special way and maybe James is giving strength to all of you. He is strong and brave. He told me last night that he wanted to watch sunsets with his son one day and I told him what a great dad he will be.

Please continue the prayers for Andrew. They headed to the beach and will stay as long as Andrew feels up to it. God bless them; give Andrew a shout on his CaringBridge site.

Please pray for JJ and Benny as well. I spoke with his brother and he said Benny had no energy. I told him the large doses of chemo were given because God knows that Benny can handle them. We are praying for many, thank you for praying for us.

Praying for James,

Jim

THURSDAY, JUNE 15, 2006 – 11:01 P.M.

"The heavens declare the glory of God; the skies proclaim the work of his hands."(Psalm 19:1)

James likes his sunsets. We watch and talk about them every evening. He always seems to find something new. When God is making them, there is always something new. He said that he hoped Andrew and JJ saw the one tonight; me too pal.

He has been feeling ok this week, he has big highs and some lows. I guess the chemo is working him over. I pray it is killing that awful cancer. We are eating a little PB&J, this time from Granma. Slowly we are trying. He sleeps well for a few hours and then he is tossing. It's strange. We pray for peaceful nights, and the sunsets help. Go out tomorrow with your kids and watch one. It makes things simple and these days, simple is what we need.

Here's to another beautiful sunset.

Praying for James,

Jim

SUNDAY, JUNE 18, 2006 – 10:48 P.M.

"How great are his signs, how mighty His wonders! His kingdom is an eternal kingdom; His dominion endures from generation to generation." (Daniel 4:3)

For someone so young, James knows just when to go out for the sunsets. We caught a great one this evening. Again, we watch and say a prayer. It was the best Father's Day ever. This family is blessed. We are trying to get to the beach next week and James told us that he just wants to sit on the beach and watch the sun do down. I think we may be able to pull that off little pal. We are in need of some relaxation. This is about the only window we will have for the summer. He has treatments starting in July and right now he feels pretty good. After a wonderful Father's day lunch with Granma and DJ, we got a call from Andrew. He invited us to the pool and away we went. James, Allison and I met his family and we had a blast. Lots of laughter and cannonballs; don't know who had the most fun, the adults or the kids. Andrew's mother called Sherry to tell how wonderful Allison was with Andrew. She is special. God graced us with her. Sherry and I don't know why we were so lucky.

Thank you for all of the guest book entries. James gets a kick out of them. Keep the prayers coming. God bless all of you and Happy Father's Day. Give your kids an extra hug and kiss and tomorrow, catch a sunset. James highly recommends them!

Praying for James,

Jim

SATURDAY, JUNE 24, 2006 – 8:27 A.M.

We are off to the beach!!! We will update next weekend. Please pray James doesn't get a fever and that he gets some great rest. Thanks for all of the prayers.

Praying for James,

Jim

THURSDAY, JULY 6, 2006 – 4:40 P.M.

"Every good and perfect gift is from above, coming down from the Father of the heavenly lights, who does not change like shifting shadows." (James 1:17)

We got that gift with our kids. I can't stress enough to love your kids and cherish each moment with them. They are a blessing from God, and please do not take them or your time with them for granted. I hear and see a lot more because of James. I thought I enjoyed life before, but since we became aware of James' illness, the world is new. I think Sherry and I were going through our life with our kids and we were having a great time. We are having a better one now. It's hard to explain; I guess that's why I say love and kiss your kids, tell folks you love them. Life is a gift and God is in control. Give Him the glory, all comes from Him.

The beach was fantastic. We had a great room on the 15th floor and a wonderful view. James liked sitting on the balcony and watching….it didn't matter the time, day or night, he liked being on the balcony. His day would vary, many times he would wake up and we would go to the beach at 6-6:30 a.m. No one was out and we found James likes the sunrise as much as the sunset. We say a prayer and he thanks Jesus for the show. He liked it when the grandparents would take him out early as well. He wouldn't do much, just walk around and watch the water. He really liked looking for sharks, and we saw five during the trip. You could see them from the balcony as they cruised the beach. They were anywhere from 3 feet to 25 feet off of the beach. Two of them were small (3-4 foot sand sharks). The biggest was on Friday a Hammerhead, 9-10 feet and was about 20 feet from shore feeding on bait fish as it swam. James found all of this cool. He saw a turtle, manta ray and numerous small rays. After an early walk we would go back to the room and he found that he liked DJ's frosted Cheerios. He has been on them since. Milk and yogurts are in, thank goodness. The two of us would settle into a chair and he would fall asleep to re-charge. He would venture down to the pool and swim for about 2 hours. It was back to the room for Cheerios and a nap. He would make it to the beach around 3:30 and stay for a while. We would go back and forth to the room, but he loved the beach. We got lots of pictures. He has a photo album and it is the most updated album on earth. He has changed the pictures more times than we can count. James loved being with Allison and she is a beach bunny. Can't get her off the beach, but going out in the water after the shark sightings was a different story. She stayed pretty close. DJ and I did get her to the second sandbar a couple of times, but she wasn't keen on the idea. She is an awesome big sis.

We got a bonus on Wednesday when their cousin, Jaclyn, was able to meet us and stay for the rest of the week. Thursday was my birthday and I had a first. James went with Granma to the store and he picked out a Power ranger cake for me. We had it for breakfast. I highly recommend that kids pick out the cakes for whatever the occasion. Very special. James told me he knew I wanted the Power Ranger cake. It said "Happy Birthday Dad and Pal." You made a great choice buddy. It was the best birthday I've ever had. The laughter, smiles and hugs were wonderful. James is feeling great and it is a joy to see him with energy. He has that sparkle in his eye. He also took the "roach" with him. It kept popping up in his Mom's purse and his sister's bed. Imagine that! We enjoy every minute. It was a great trip; we needed the time off and the time together.

Thank you for all of the prayers. We need them all. We got James on more prayer lists. He is on from North Caroline to Ohio to Texas. Thanks to everyone. Please keep Andrew in your prayers. He goes to the hospital today. Please keep JJ and Benny in your prayers as well. There are a lot of people that need some extra love. It doesn't hurt, and is very rewarding. We continue to ask Jesus for his blessings; not only for us, but all of you as well.

Praying for James,

Jim

MONDAY, JULY 10, 2006 – 10:27 P.M.

"But I trust in you, O Lord; I say, "You are my God." My times are in your hands…" (Psalm 31:14-15)

Our time is in His hands and it is comforting. How truly thankful we are. We know our trial is not an enemy of our faith, but an opportunity to prove God's faithfulness. I know Jesus is in control and He is the ultimate doctor and healer. He is working through all of the wonderful people at Children's (Hospital) and we are blessed. Once again, we give Him the glory.

James and I have been on our own since Friday. Sherry and Allison are in Orlando at national dance competition. This was planned last August and James and I were to be at the parks while they danced, but we had a little detour. It's ok; we will make it soon to see Mickey and the gang. James wasn't very happy to see them leave and it was very tough on Mom. We agreed that she had to go for Allison because Dad sure couldn't do hair and makeup. That would've been a mess. They will be back July 13. I have to brag on Allison, she was in competition with 13 girls in her age group Saturday. She came in 1st! She won $500 and a big trophy. Sherry said she didn't know how she would get the trophy home. I am so proud of her, all that is going on with her brother and she is able to keep focused. I don't know what we did to deserve the wonderful kids we have. I am honored to be their Dad, they are a gift and I love them more each day.

James has been feeling pretty well. He has some double vision, but it clears up after he eats. He has been on peanut butter and crackers since Friday. Any protein is good in my eyes. We have to get his weight up for our visit on the 12th, because we know his appetite will go down when he starts chemo. We start cycle 5 of 9. We spend the night and go through the process. I hate this because of how he feels from 5 weeks off, but we have a course we must follow. We continue to have faith that we are going through this for reasons that one day will be known.

We went bowling Saturday and he bowled a 101. Pretty good. He helped me clean Mon's car, do some laundry and we watched movies. He went to see his cousins "bad boys" (boxer puppies) Sunday. James had dog spit all over his face and he loved it. He spent the night at the grandparents last night. It was too quiet at the house and I couldn't sleep. He and I will get ready for our visit. He knows what is coming and he tells me he is going to be alright. He's always comforting everyone around him. My "pal" is awesome. We are going toy shopping for our hospital stay. Goodness knows what he will get; my guess is something in the Cars or Power Ranger department.

Please pray that the chemos do their job and we don't have any of the bad stuff. He has tolerated them well so far, but we haven't been off this long between treatments. Thanks to all for praying for my buddy, he needs and deserves every one of them. He is so tough and strong; please pray for his strength to continue. He is my hero, and teaches me more about loving life each day.

We continue our sunset time. Take one in, you won't be disappointed. I see James pointing things out to me when we are travelling and then in that beautiful voice of his I hear, "thanks Jesus." You are right buddy, thank you Jesus for loving us.

Our friend started his stem cell treatments over the weekend, please pray for him. There are many more, so please take time out of your day to lift them up and thank our Lord for His grace.

Praying for James,

Jim

SUNDAY, JULY 16, 2006 – 9:15 P.M.

"Jesus said…"If you believe, you will receive whatever you ask for in prayer." (Matthew 21:22)

We keep asking and believing and He delivers. We give Him all of the glory. We are blessed.

James has been feeling great since his treatment last Wednesday. Dr. Reddy said, "James, you look like a million bucks." That was all I need to hear. James did all she asked and we got our room for the night. James took everything in stride and was a great patient. He still doesn't understand why they wake him up every couple of hours. Me either, pal. He was very happy to see Mom and Allison on Thursday. Sherry was worried about us, but Granma and DJ took up the slack. His appetite has dropped off, but the prayers on not getting sick are answered. We are confident the appetite will return, we just don't know what it will be. Right now its yogurts, milk, cheese Pringles and a little toast. We keep praying for a normal day. One day, it will come.

Please keep praying for James and all of his friends that are sick. This is an ugly and hateful thing James is going through, but through the grace of God, he will be cured. Thank you for all the prayers and thoughts, they are comforting. We are on the down slide for treatments, but we still have a long way to go. Thanks for going through this journey with us.

Praying for James,

Jim

WEDNESDAY, JULY 19, 2006 – 9:47 P.M.

"He is not far from each one of us." (Acts 17:27)

We feel His power all around us, He gives us the strength we need and we are thankful and blessed. I'm glad Jesus is in control.

Another great visit for James. Dr. Reddy said he looked great, his counts had not changed and he lost 2 oz. They were very happy about both. The blood work shocked them, because it hadn't changed from the week before and they had increased his chemo. He keeps surprising them and we give all of the glory to God. James took everything in stride. One more week and we have three off. Looking forward to that. James came home and ate 6 pieces of bacon and a chocolate shake. The docs say anything he eats is great and keeping an appetite so soon after treatment is wonderful. Thanks for checking in on James. He just asked why I did this update (on the computer) and I told him that lots of people check on him everyday and say prayers for him. I wish you could see the smile. It is a very welcomed sight. Please keep the prayers going, we need them. Give your kids some extra love tonight, they deserve it. Thanks to all and God bless.

Praying for James,

Jim

SUNDAY, JULY 23, 2006 – 10:17 P.M.

Just a quick note, it's getting late and we are tired. James is feeling great. His appetite isn't where we would like, but he is showing that he wants to eat. We will find something. He came to me last night right before he was going to bed and showed me the sunset out of the bathroom window. He said, "Jesus gave us pinks and purples." Awesome. I think his counts are going down a little because he is getting cold and wants to be outside. We go back Wednesday and finish cycle 5. We are ready to get this over with. Please continue the prayers. James has a laugh that fills the house, it is wonderful to hear. He is running around and is like he was before this started. Please keep praying for his demeanor to continue. His smile and laughter are infectious. Please pray for all of our friends fighting this disease, they need all of us.

Praying for James,

Jim

WEDNESDAY, JULY 26, 2006 – 9:32 P.M.

"But by faith we eagerly await through the Spirit the righteousness for which we hope." (Galatians 5:5)

There are times when things aren't going good and darkness seems to be around. Waiting is hard, but it reveals hope. We wait and wait, and seem to have an empty place in our heart, and yet we don't allow it to be filled with anything less than the best God has to offer. I guess that is patience. Jesus gives us our greatest strength when he teaches us to wait for hope. I guess that was His hope when He prayed in the Garden the last night He had on this earth. We are thankful He shows us the way and that is His will. We give Him all of the glory.

Today was the end of cycle 5 and James passed with flying colors. Dr. Spiller (Dr. Reddy's new doctor) saw James today and said he "looked tremendous and we'll see you in 3 weeks." Wonderful words to hear. James was laughing so much that Dr. Reddy's PA, Allison, opened the door and said, "What is going on in here? I can hear you laugh down the hall." James gave her that smile of his and she just laughed. You could tell that they liked seeing him and hearing him as much as us. I guess they don't get a lot of that in Clinic 8, but James was glad to help them out. He gained a pound from last week, (thank you bacon) and for the first time in his young life, he weights 40 pounds. Dr. Reddy liked that. She saw James in the hall and told him his boots (black cowboy with silver chains/spurs) were "outstanding." James likes her compliments. Angela and "Clay" stopped by as were leaving and James had to show him his new Transformer. "Clay" was impressed. I can't tell you how wonderful and special Angela is. Not only to our family, but so many others. God will continue to bless that special lady and her "friend." Since this started she has taken so much stress off of James. I really don't know how we would have gotten James to do some of the things he had to do, but Angela and 'Clay" could talk him into just about anything. If "Clay" could get James to put on a hospital gown that showed his booty, he could get him to do most anything! We are grateful to them for taking heart wrenching and tough situations for James and making them bearable.

Again we are blessed to have them in our corner. James and Allison stopped by TCBY and James had vanilla with m&ms. Sherry said there was nothing left. His appetite is pretty good this soon after a treatment and we are thankful. They told us to watch him and if he starts running out of energy to stop by and get his blood checked. If last night was an indicator, we won't be stopping by. We were on the basketball court for about an hour hitting the baseball. He was swinging better than he has all year. We saw our sunset and it was a great day. Jesus continues to smile on us and we are thankful. It's all of the prayers. Thanks to everyone.

Praying for James,

Jim

MONDAY, JULY 31, 2006 – 9:31 P.M.

"For I am the Lord, your God, who takes hold of your right hand and says to you, do not fear; I will help you." (Isaiah 41:13)

That is how we get through the day. We know who is in charge. We are blessed and thankful. I go back to what Dr. Satchivi (James' surgeon) said. "You're in for a marathon, not a sprint." With God holding your son's hand, how can we be afraid? James isn't.

We've had a good week. James if feeling good and while we want his appetite to get better and open up to other foods, we have to sit back and relax and know Jesus is in his heart and knows what is best.

Friday afternoon James and I made it to the store to pick out Granma's birthday cake. James did not disappoint me and he picked out a "Pirates of the Caribbean" cake. It was awesome and Saturday night Granma was beaming; it was a first for her on cake! Uncle Len stopped by with "Lexie" and the "Bad Boys." (Havanese and Boxer pups). James was in heaven with 4 dogs. When Maximus and Bentley would chase each other and run headfirst into the coffee table or sofa James would have tears running down his face from laughing. He had dog spit all over his face. Allison and Jaclyn made up a dance and the performance was on! Birthdays have become a little more special for all of us.

We made it to church as a family for the first time in a while. The service was on "signs." We have them all around us. When the minister was speaking I looked at Sherry and she was crying. I think she finally "let go" and she knows that Jesus has this. I told her the day we found out about James that he was in a "win, win." He stays with us, or he goes home with Jesus. I'm at peace and I think now she is. Yes, it's very tough to think that way, but it is the truth. That doesn't mean we will stop fighting for James, we just are pointed on the path that He is leading. His will, not ours. There are many other kids fighting, and we pray for them daily. I've said this before, but we are blessed. I pray all of you never have to experience your world changing, so please love your kids and give them an extra kiss and hug, read them that extra book, overlook the little things, watch a sunset, stay a little longer at the pool, let them win, don't put off anything with your kids and say, "Let's do that tomorrow." Do it now and live and love through them. I know it's easy to say find the time, but tough to do, but look into the face of the child that God blessed you with and tell them "yes" to whatever is on that beautiful little mind, … …and tell them you love them. May God bless all of you. Thank you for praying for our son.

Remember to pray for our little friend, Andrew, also JJ, Benny and so many others.

Praying for James,

Jim

MONDAY, AUGUST 7, 2006 – 8:56 P.M.

"You hear, O Lord, the desire of the afflicted; you encourage them, and you listen to their cry…" (Psalm 10:17)

We are thankful that He listens. Sometimes we can't hear Him, but He is always there. There is a lot of suffering, with many families, but it is comforting to know that Jesus is in control of all situations.

James has been feeling good. The last couple of days he has slowed. He is napping a little more and his appetite isn't great, but we think it's his counts going down. Hopefully before we go back (8/23), he will rally. You can see that he wants to get more active, his stamina comes and goes. When he has it, he rocks, we played ball on the b-ball courts the other night with a bunch of Allison's friends. He liked playing ball with the "guys." He ran harder than ever and was wiped out when we made it home for a shower. Saturday night James was the man of the hour for a party. Several 8th grade girls got together for a swim party to celebrate their birthdays and instead of presents they pick a cause and donate the money. This year it was for James and The Janie Sims Foundation. The parents of those girls are very proud. I would be. It was wonderful and generous and in today's age, a breath of fresh air. James swam like a fish and had a great time. We made it to see "Barnyard." James and Skittles, a great combination. We have added (links to their CaringBridge websites) more kids that need your prayers. Again, thank you for praying for James. Sometimes we feel really good, and then we read about others and the reality of our situation is brought home. Please love and hug your kids. They deserve it. Don't put anything on hold, or do it tomorrow. Go play ball or read that book. We all benefit. You can see them, and Jesus, smile.

Praying for James

Jim

THURSDAY, AUGUST 10, 2006 – 8:45 P.M.

"But let all who take refuge in you be glad; let them ever sign for joy. Spread your protection over them, that those who love your name may rejoice in you." (Psalm 5:11)

We are protected; He is watching over James.

There is something about a little boy, running around the room with underwear on his head that is pulled down over one eye, yelling ARRGH! like a pirate, that brings a smile to your face. We are blessed. James has had a good day. Wish they would stay like this. Soon, hopefully, soon. As you can guess, he feels good. He started off the day with Cap'n Crunch and milk, French fries at noon, 2 eggs in the early afternoon and he finished it off with milk and for the first time since October and this nightmare began, 1 ½ chicken fingers. I had a tear in my eye when he ate them. You just go back to when things were "normal." One day, one day. It was a huge day for him, he found out who his kindergarten teacher is. We look forward to a wonderful year with Mrs. Jost. We kind of got a jump on things, and James was excited to be in the room. He goes tomorrow for a little while and sees everyone in his class and Monday is the first day. Allison was happy with her teacher as well, and like she says, "Dad, give me lemons and I'll make lemonade." We are blessed to have her. She has been unbelievable through all of this. We plan on taking it easy this weekend.

Praying for James,

Jim

MONDAY, AUGUST 14, 2006 – 9:07 P.M.

"The important thing is that in every way, whether from false motives or true, Christ is preached. And because of this I rejoice. Yes, and I will continue to rejoice, but I know that through your prayers and the help given by the Spirit of Jesus Christ, what has happened to me will turn out for my deliverance." (Philippians 1:18-19)

If this is the reason for our trial, then His word will be spread. We are giving God all of the glory for James. We feel all of the prayers, and God is smiling. Come see my son, you will see what I mean.

Last November we did not know what the future held. Sherry said she hoped he could just make kindergarten. His first full day was today. He had a blast. Sherry said he got in the car and didn't stop talking about this day. It was great to hear, Jesus is smiling on him. Lunch was early and I don't think his PB&J thawed. James said it was "crunchy." Bless his heart. They were out on the playground a lot and in this heat, I thought he would wilt, but he didn't. He took a nap and Mrs. Jost said several of the kids took advantage of the sleepy time. Sherry said he was eating fries and chocolate milk while they waited on Allison's carpool. She had a wonderful day as well. Jesus is showering his blessings on us. We give thanks, not only to Him, but to all of you who lift James up daily with prayer. It is very powerful, and we are humbled. Please don't take today for granted, make school a big deal for them. Take the time to hear about their day. It's important to them. We weren't sure we would have this day; once again, He is smiling on us. We say "Thanks Jesus," for today and your sunsets. God bless all of you.

Praying for James,

Jim